# A Pocketful of Verse

## and other compositions

In appreciation of Simsbury's hospitality as personified by my dear friend August

*Photograph by Herb Snitzer*

# *A Pocketful of Verse* and other compositions of

## Robert J. Lurtsema

**Parnassus Imprints**
**Orleans, Massachusetts**

ISBN 0-949160-50-1

Library of Congress Catalogue number 91-061710

8/3/92

Herald photo by Lou Ball

SISTER CITY EXHIBIT — An exhibit of photographs and memorabilia of the Berlin Wall opened last week at the Simsbury Library under the auspices of the "Wittmund Sister City" group and the German Embassy in Boston. Taking part in the opening were, left to right, Margitta Dahlberg, a native of Berlin; Librarian Joanne Pierce; Paul G. Stein; Barbara and Tido Holtkamp; Elise Sirman; and poet Robert Lurtsema. The exhibit is on display the rest of the month.

To my mother

Dorothy Veronica Catugno Lurtsema

and my father

John Sietsa Lurtsema

## ❧ Author's Preface

Welcome! This is our book. Yours because you're reading it. Mine because I wrote it. And I'm delighted to be sharing it with you.

This is a book of verse and, more specifically, about verse. It is a book about words: the brush strokes of verse, the clay of poetry.

As a chronological accounting, it is a sketchbook of experiences, highlighting the many ways in which verse has been an influence in my life. In that sense, this book is a journey over a period of more than five decades, a trip I've already taken.

Along the way there is love, life and death, pathos, happiness, tragedy, humor and the eternal struggle of an incipient idea seeking its ultimate expression. I've included a little of what I've learned as I stumbled through this course, along with much of what I am still trying to learn. And I couldn't resist an occasional touch of whimsy.

The book was fun to put together and I wanted it to be fun for you too. I hope it is.

Whether the journey is short or long
One could do much worse
Than to take along
A happy song
And a pocketful of verse

The J stands for John.

I didn't have a middle name when I was born—just Robert Lurtsema. A trochee followed by a dactyl. As a child, I knew nothing about metric feet; only that the name seemed somehow to be lacking a syllable.

The solution was Confirmation, one of the many barely comprehensible rituals that was part of my religious upbringing. My sister Jacqueline, younger than I by a year, and I went through it together. But this time it was different.

It meant I could choose a middle name. And I was excited by the prospect. My father's name was John, and that's what I chose.

I always thought the picture looked more like a bride and groom.

I chose the name John, but mostly what I wanted was the middle initial, and the comfortable cadence of that double dactyl.

Higgledy piggledy
Dactylic merriment
Moving in rhythm with
Robert J. Lurtsema
Jumpin' Jehoshaphat
Isn't it grand

Later (although I couldn't have guessed it then), it would march through a couple of decades right in step with that other double dactyl, Morning pro musica.

It's surprising how often I'm asked what the J stands for. But that's something I don't mind. When I answer, I always think of my father, and all that he stood for. "He was a man—taken for all in all, I shall not look upon his like again." He had a knack for rhyme, and as his first-born son, I was a big event.

## ❧ To My Pal Bobby

*by John S. Lurtsema*

I've a common tale to tell,
And I hope I tell it well,
It's the reason for my constant pride and joy.
I've been this way every day,
Since my wife to me did say,
"Daddy dear, our little baby is a boy."

Every morning he's awake,
Crying, "Daddy, come and take,"
And I must get up and take him or he'll cry.
But he's such a little dear,
That his each and every tear,
Lets me know that if I lost him I would die.

When he's dressed and had his food,
Then he's not so very good,
Full of mischief like I want to see a boy,
And no matter what his pranks,
He knows his daddy never spanks,
For to daddy he is nothing but a joy.

All day long we watch him play,
Till his nap takes him away,
To the blessed land of all good babies' dreams
And we try to plan a new
Thing to teach him how to do
While he sleeps we plan some new and
better schemes.

And when evening's drawing nigh
And our baby starts to cry
Then there isn't any more to be said
I must part then with my pal
Say good night then, 'cause I shall
Have to kiss his cheek and tuck him into bed.

□

***My father and I looked so much alike that everyone was convinced this was a photograph of me.***

Dad was a carpenter—a designer—a builder. He had sure hands, that did what he wanted them to do. There were always tools around, which I quickly learned to use, putting nails in bureaus and sawing table legs.

Sometimes (for my mother's peace of mind) I was taken to the job where I was kept busy pulling the nails out of the scrap lumber in between stacking and hauling and cleaning up. Years later I had learned enough to work along with the crew on roofing, sidewalls, repairs; we even built complete houses from the foundation up.

Sometimes my father would recite a new verse to me, which I would secretly memorize. I'm not sure about the authorship of the following. My mother doesn't remember it at all. But I remember clearly his reciting it to me, except for the fourth line. I added that later, although I'm not so sure now that adding the middle rhyme adds anything to the verse.

## ❧ Life

Life is as you make it
From the day you're born
In this world you're thrown
Then you're on your own
Till your life is worn
And death doth take it.

□

My father was a gentle, hard working, powerful man, with an easy smile. Very much in charge, and yet always amiable, he was an easy man to like. Unschooled but not unskilled, his ability to create set the example for me, or maybe it was in the genes. He didn't write verse often, but when he did, and shared it with me, it was a kinship that was special beyond words.

His natural leadership carried him to high posts in the Masons and the Veterans of Foreign Wars. On those occasions when I, still a pre-teen, was allowed to read one of his verses or prayers at a meeting or service, it was a time of great pride.

One of his poems that made a significant and lasting impression on me was a ballad called "The Tramp's Dream."

## ❧ The Tramp's Dream

*by John S. Lurtsema*

The night was cold and dreary
The rain was falling fast
And all about the village
None were gay as in the past.

In the corner of a doorway
Where the flooring still was dry
Lay the body of a maiden
Death had sent to Him on high.

As I looked, it seemed to shiver
And I rubbed my eyes in vain
Still that body dead forever
Shook as though 'twere feeling pain.

I gently knelt beside the maiden
And with hands now icy cold
I tried to touch the shaking body
But her features could not behold.

I awoke as dawn was breaking
Sitting upright in my bed
And found with heart nigh on to breaking
My wife beside me lying dead.

The Lord had shown me in my slumber
What I would find when I awoke
So now I tramp the world all over
Never happy, always broke.

Now I guess I'll leave you brethren
And keep walking while I can
If my prayers are heard above me
She and I will meet again.

□

Fortunately, The Tramp's Dream was only fiction. My mother was very much alive.

And very beautiful.

And they loved each other very much.

And I guess I was pretty lovable too . . . at first.

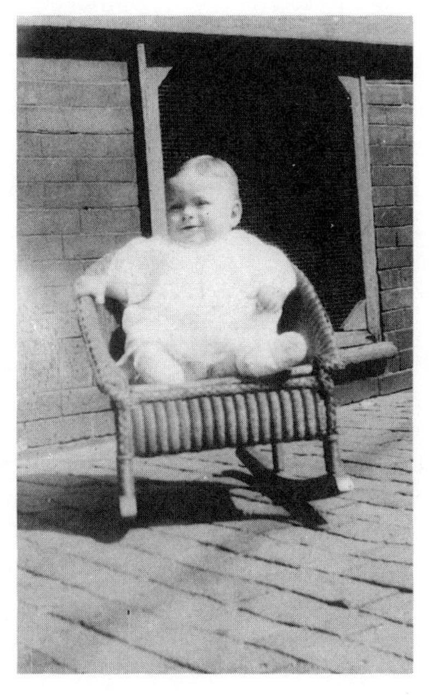

Put me on a pony
To pose for a picture
And I was a paragon
Of perfect peace and poise.

□

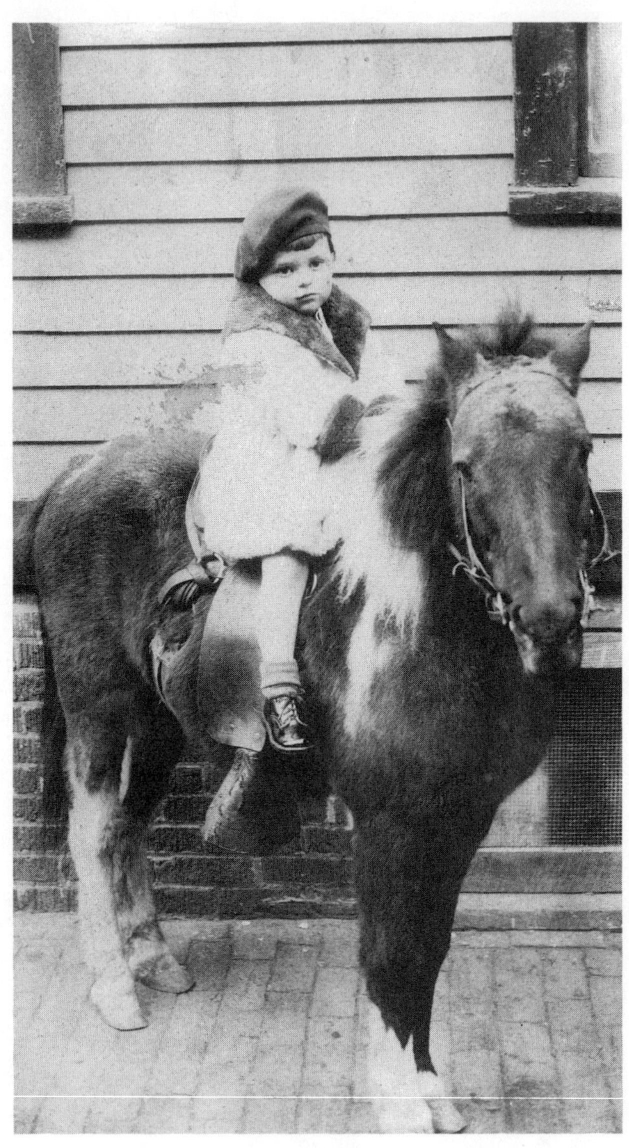

***in winter***

***and in summer***

But the pony came around only twice a year and the rest of the time I was relentlessly energetic. Behind that angelic exterior dwelt a demon of insatiable curiosity. I wanted to know what made everything work.

If anyone was around I would ask "How?" If they didn't know, I'd ask "Why?" And if no one was around, I'd take it apart to find out for myself.

It was years before I developed any interest in putting things back together.

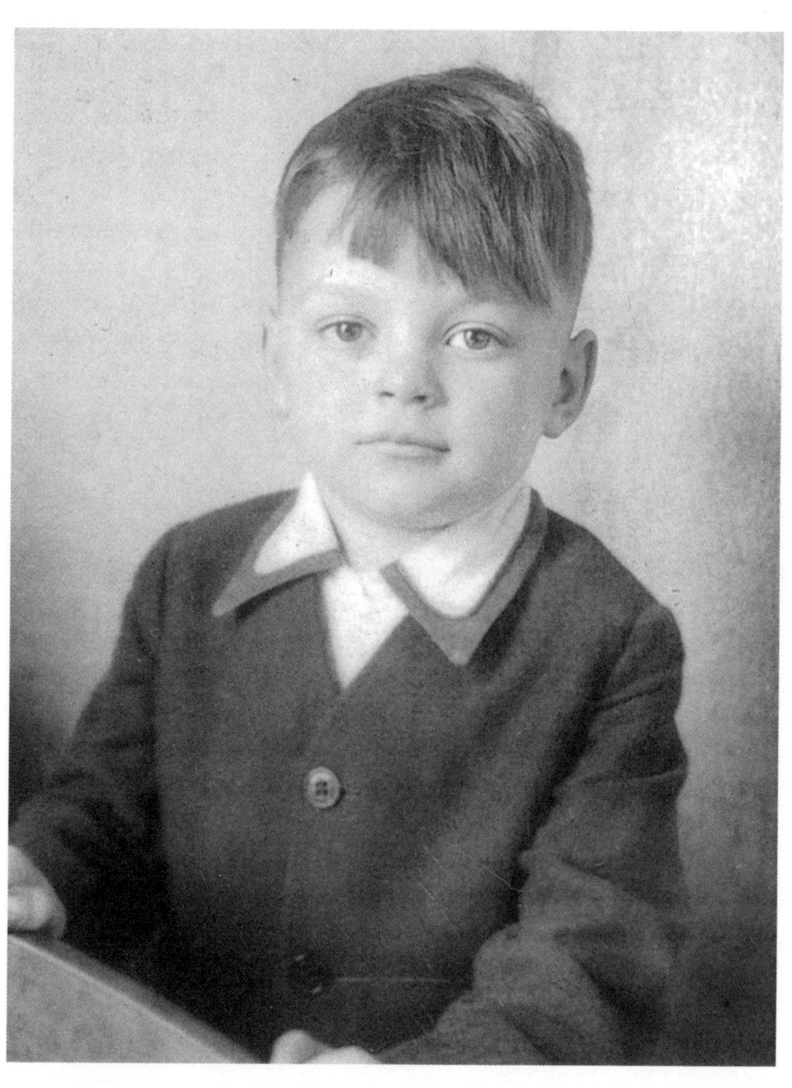

I was a natural explorer. Every new vista was an avenue to adventure, every venue a chance for new discoveries. I was fascinated with what things were called, and how they went together, which bird made which sound, how it flew and where it nested.

Trees had a special appeal, usually from as high up as I could climb, and especially as I learned to recognize them by name, even in winter. I learned the names of stars and stones and shells and weeds. I was a model student everywhere except at school.

My forays into the great outdoors served to get me out from underfoot, a blessing that was offset by the fact that I was almost never home on time.

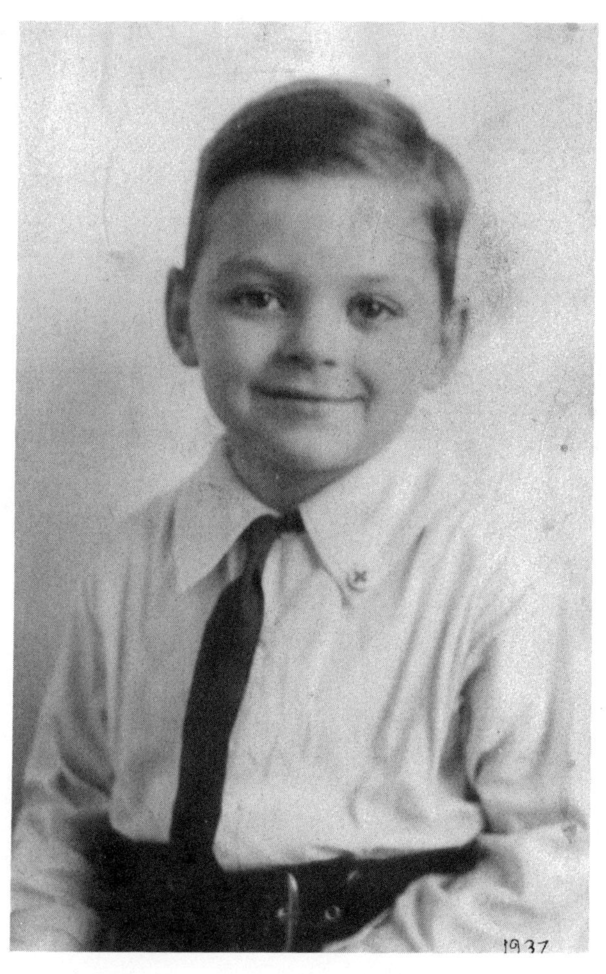
1937

My first attempts at rhyme made a quick passage through "cute" followed by a lengthy journey into "annoying." They served to entertain my peers and irritate everyone else. Then (probably to everyone's relief), I stopped. Or seemed to. Actually, I had found a new game, a greater challenge.

I would spend entire days talking in rhyme, but in such a way as to escape detection. This meant choosing rhyme schemes of varying complexity depending on who was listening. For the kids, a simple ABAB pattern was usually sufficient. But with adults, it was much more difficult.

About this same time, I developed a passion for reading, which, probably as much as anything, helped to preserve my mother's sanity.

My mother was only 17 when I was born. She was prepared for motherhood, but not necessarily for me. It was the depths of the Depression. Times were not easy, and I didn't make them any easier. I was learning how to cope with life, and she was learning how to cope with me.

It was my own increasingly urgent need to create that made things easier for both of us. Every hour of building, writing, painting was another hour of peace. For both of us. Drawing and painting came as easily to me as rhyme. I finished my first serious landscape, a watercolor of deer and mountains at dawn, when I was eight.

School was a special challenge—for my teachers, as well as for me. It wasn't that I wasn't interested in what was being taught as much as that what was being taught wasn't what I was interested in.

I graduated from Boston English High School when I was 15, thanks to the city's double promotion system, which was how they moved the brighter pupils into the next higher grade. In my case, I think it was more that my curiosity led me to ask more questions than were thought of by the rest of the students. And, of course, it also gave the teachers the opportunity to get me out of their class. Unfortunately, getting a couple of double promotions meant that there was a lot of basic information that I never got taught.

If school was a challenge, homework was even more so. Even though I had been rhyming for years, I was 13 before I wrote my first poem. It didn't rhyme, and it wasn't what I was supposed to write.

I had been given an assignment to write an essay on some topic of so little interest that I can't remember what it was, but instead my mind started toying around with the concept of "Now." Having nothing else to show for my night's labors, I turned it in, and to my surprise, got an A minus.

Having been thus rewarded, I was hooked.

## ❧ Now

I used to think when I said
Now
That it had gone
And so it never was
Nor could I then anticipate
Another chance at Now
For fear it would have been.
But since that time
A myriad of Nows
Have gathered up and aged me
And with that growth
Came knowledge of one truth:
There is a present
Though the past never was
And the future never can be.
For each fleet-footed moment
Before it sprouts a wing upon its heel
And flees,
For the sake of that one moment
Is Now
And never can be changed.
This makes "past" and "future"
Words in pretty sayings
Or thoughts
In silly contrast to each other.
And if this "then" and "when"
Can have no meaning
The only thing I need consider
Now
Is Now.

□

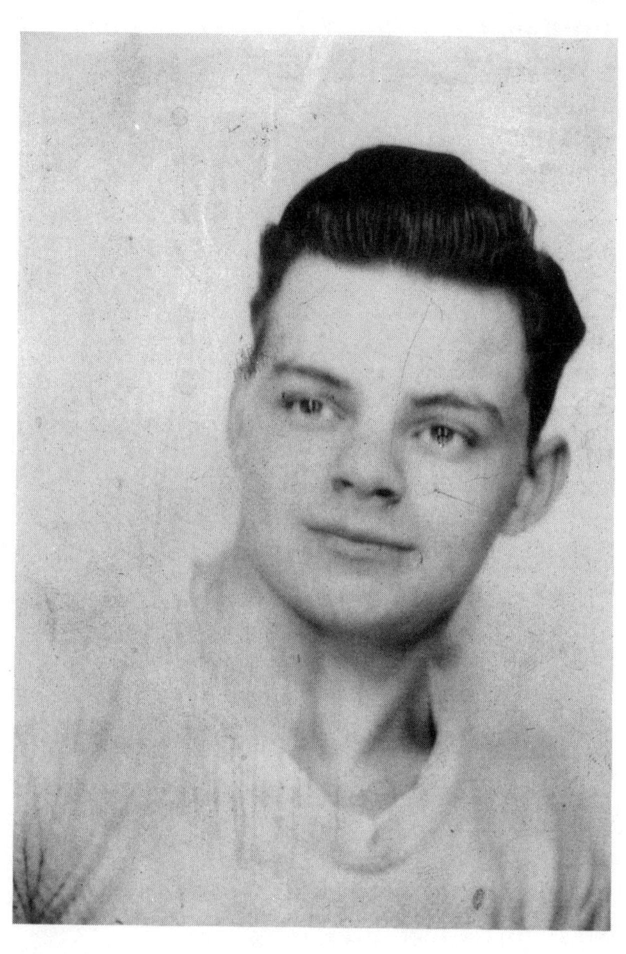

As it turned out, talking in rhyme was easier than writing it. You'd think they'd be the same; but there's something about seeing the word on the printed page that makes you want to change it. It's analogous to writing a speech or just telling someone about something. Talking is ephemeral.

I wrote a lot of stuff that wasn't worth saving, but it was good practice. And the practice paid off.

My mother's patience was rewarded with a poem about her that won first prize, complete with ceremony and even our picture in the paper. Maybe motherhood was worth it, after all.

BOSTON POST, MONDAY MAY 12, 1947

# Boy's Poem, "Mother," Wins Prize at Program

POETRY CONTEST WINNER

Robert J. Lurtsema, 11, with his mother, Mrs. Dorothy Lurtsema, at Burroughs Newsboys Foundation, where the boy won first prize for his Mother's Day poem.

---

Robert J. Lurtsema, 15, of 33 Circuit st., Roxbury, was awarded first prize for his poem entitled, "Mother," at the annual Mother's Day exercises yesterday afternoon at the Burroughs Newsboys Foundation, 15 Somerset st., Beacon Hill.

## ❧ Mother

The winds of greed
The storms of hate
The clouds of sorrow
Pass our gate

But through the windows
In the house of love
One still can see
In the heavens above

A ray of sunshine
That bursts through the haze
And breaks its way
To earth through a maze

Of infinite space
Finally to fall
On one person here
The greatest of all.

In spite of the darkness
There's always this light
To guide us along
And to teach us what's right

To take us on trips
To the fair in the town
And to bring us a smile
To abolish our frown.

For unselfish love
I'll not find another
As sweet nor as kind
As my lovable mother.

□

Having justified my mother's faith, I was ready to tackle the problems of the world.

A friend, who at 17 was a year older than I, was having difficulty relating to her mother. The verse for children that I wrote in response to her problem was an allegory that I hoped might help.

## ❧ The Wall

*a verse for children*

There stood a sturdy, stolid wall
between two raging seas
and all
the pleas
on either side,
the breathing swells, persistent tide
but left that wall undaunted.

Each year were borne new hurricanes
and crushed against the stone
the rains
were thrown
with such a force
that for that wall
there seemed no course
but yield and fall.
Still, more than this was wanted.

Even battering, hammering storms;
winter, spring, fall,
unending scorch of searing summer heat
all
met defeat,
could not bring down that wall.

Way down below where the water was green
and livin' was happy 'cause life was clean
a little fish
ever so small
encountered the wall
and thought it was great
a new playmate
and he rubbed up against the wall,
and it felt so good
on his little scaled hood
that he rubbed some more on the wall
on the big, strong, sturdy, stubborn wall
for nothing ever matched
the way the mortar scratched
and eased the awful itching
in his every little scale.

He wriggled
and he wiggled
and flicked his frisky tail
at the wall
at the huge and heavy, hovering wall
that would not fall.

When time to play
ended with the day
the little fish never,
ever at all
swam very far away
but always returned
where his little heart yearned
to be
in the sea

by the wall,
by the old and obdurate,
but weakened
wall.

For the wall had no protection
from so much affection
and soon the fish wore through
and he swam back and forth from sea to sea
as gleefully
as a fish could be
swimming through a wall.

As the little fish grew,
as all fishes do,
the hole did too
and so did the action of the sea.
The little flow
that had started slow
began to grow
as the wall wavered dangerously.

A loss of strength
a wave-forced quiver
along its length
a mighty shiver
then torn asunder
a heavy splash
of watered thunder
and muffled crash.

Down to the ocean's floor went ton upon ton
and two seas above rolled together as one. □

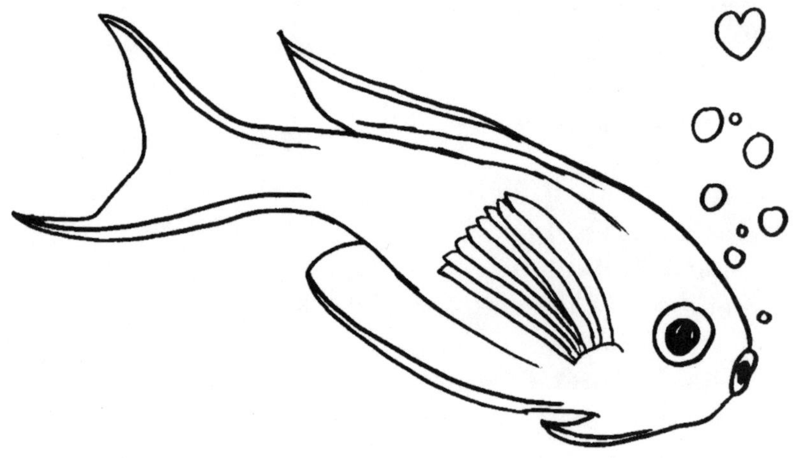

My father and I were Navy men. He served in the First World War and I was in during the Korean conflict. I think we both looked pretty good in uniform.

***Dad***

***me***

Compared to the Navy, school had been a piece of cake. In an ultra-regimented society where conformity is everything, I was a maverick misfit.

Fortunately, I got into Special Services in French Morocco, running a radio station, a newspaper, a photo lab, and a drama club, and felt much more at home. Now my knack for rhyme came in handy in many ways, not the least of which was entertaining the troops with lusty limericks, ribald rhymes, or epic ballads on trivial topics.

## ❧ Ode to A.A.

Now, our minds are schooled on grief and death,
And our lips must be aware. . .
But our feet still seek a railing
When there is no railing there.

My heart is all resigned and calm.
So likewise is my soul,
But my habituated foot
Is quite beyond control.

I stood inside the grocery store
Buying stamps and soap.
My foot rose up in spite of me
And pawed the air with hope.

I'll find no winds from east nor west,
Nor gusty squalls about
To raise a welcome cloud and pour
Relief upon this drought.

Nor will these winds return to me
When quieted and spiced
With scents of drinks that used to be.
Can I hang on? Oh Christ!

No glass shall greet my straining eyes
No matter how they blink.
My ears shall never hear again
The whiskey glasses clink.

There isn't anywhere a jug
To cuddle with my wrist,
But my habituated foot
Remains an optimist.

It lifts itself, it curls itself
It feels the empty air,
And it seeks a long brass railing
When there is no railing there.

Now I don't ask your sympathy
For my throat or bloodshot eyes,
Nor stomach fraught with unquenched thirst,
Nor my liver's painful cries.

And I don't ask your pity for
My tongue with taste denied,
Nor do I seek your tears because
My lips are shrunk and dried.

But, Oh my foot! My cheated foot!
My foot that lives in hope!
Oh, what a piteous sight, to see
It lift itself and grope.

I look at it. I talk to it.
I chastise it and plead.
But, with a humble cheerfulness
That makes my heart to bleed,

It lifts itself, it curls itself,
It searches through the air!
And it seeks a long brass railing
When there is no railing there.

To church, I took this foot of mine,
Oh foot! So fond and frail.
I had to drag it back in haste.
It grabbed the chancel rail.

My heart is all resigned and calm
So, likewise, is my soul,
But my habituated foot
Is quite beyond control.

Climbing up a flight of stairs,
And wishing for a nip,
My foot reached up and clutched the rail
And crushed it in its grip.

It grabs the footrail of my bunk
With such determined clasp,
That I am forced to strike the thing
To make it lose its grasp.

Sometimes, it leaps to clutch the curb
When I walk down the street.
Oh! How I suffer for the hope
That lives within my feet.

Myself, I can endure the drought
With stoic calm and prayer
But my foot still seeks a railing
And, there is no railing there.

□

After the Navy, it was off to college, where, as any serious student knows, the pursuit of knowledge is often subordinate to other pursuits.

## ❧ To Norma

Who was it
put the whale in a glass of water,
and bade it swim around?
Not me!
Because I knew there wasn't room
and I'm a practical man.

You asked me
what love means to me
and I was quick to answer
lest my hesitation prove
I had not found an answer for myself.
Thoughts, too fast,
and all confused,
colliding, the concussion
of dark green splashed on white.
Or
thoughts, furiously certain,
strangling with a plea
for room to grow
and time to reach maturity.

The ant that climbs
the elephant's leg
with dreams of rape
has more humility
than clumsy, base and blundering man
who gives to God a definition
or tries to translate
the color of peach
into the collar of words.

I watched the ashen emptiness of morning
blush with the thought of revealing day
and hid my head in shame
because I know the worthiness
of truth
and yet have curled my tongue
around the tempting candy cane
of lies.

Will the smooth rounded rim of the glass
cut through the hide,
through the barnacled whaleskin?

And you,
who strive to thwart yourself
by denying the existence
of the certitude you seek
would have me desecrate my love
by branding it on apathetic air
with heated words.
I saw the corners of your lips
curl down past naked upper teeth,
eyes wide and whitened with disdain,
and cringed
in the hollow grey of loneliness.
When the last corrugated sob
had rasped the coarse wool coating
of my desiccated throat,
I still had not discovered
the meaning of my love
but only ascertained
its perspicacity,
abysmally profound,
yet enigmatic.

Across the slippery bottom
of an ordinary tumbler
slides the belly of a whale.
But not the tail. Not yet, the tail.

Trapped within the kaleidoscope
of time
life is cut
by bits of shattered glass.
Cold insensitive edges
slice an ever changing pattern
mirrored on itself.
No order, no cause, no system,
only the chaos of change.
And inside this snare of time
life whirls from sickened yellow-green
to warm dull orange.

Reunion is a time for joy
but first must stand the test
of recomparing values.
The greatest justification for living
is the ability to share.

Our minds are vines
twined in mutual support
and climbing upward into light
sharing the dreams of flight
and yet accepting the existence
of roots that hold us
down to earth.
Once torn apart
we can no longer grow,

but holding together
and fed by the earth
we can soar above the other vines
to share a greater portion of the world.

Our minds are equally dissatisfied
with slowly changing patterns.
For us, the bits of glass
must spin a new design
with ever increasing acceleration
or we grow restless.

We both seek to understand,
and use our understanding to create.
We both refuse to sacrifice
the accomplishment
of conscious originality,
and yet can teach each other
and learn together.
We reject a life that's hewn
by the demands of everyday existence.
We anticipate a life that's filled
with opportunities
to interpret and appreciate
aesthetic experience.

We both enjoy the feeling
of a raw world
pressed against our naked flesh,
fertile, verdant, and unhampered
by the clumsy handiwork of man.
We share a mutual contempt
for concupiscience
and still find satisfaction in the sensual.
Hot breath on searching tongues
and the rusty sunset of your hair
when your cheekbone finds
a snuggled softness in warm flesh
between my chest and shoulder.
If ever the kaleidoscope of time
should stop its silly spinning
and set the fragments of life
into a constant color pattern
let it be the warmth of this one moment.
One short glimpse
assuring us both
of the attainability of certitude,
the world I choose to call truth,
the need you feel
for what you cannot give a name to
and so convince yourself
that it does not exist.

Then from the moonstained sheen
of a worn out sea
a thin dead echo beckons
"Lead me—where others cannot see."
But I am lonely, leading,
and I do not know the way.
Together, walking side by side,
we can share the view.
But, alone, I stumble,
blinded by the loss of you.
I will not block your vision
and accept the dubious glory of leader
by relegating you
to the sightless role of follower.

If this is the shroud
that time decrees
for partnership,
then time
has no more right than I to progress.
Bring back the one moment of warmth
rich, ripe, red, gold.
Kill this clammy blackness.
Order time to halt.
Stop growth.
And fight against tomorrow.

And derision grins at me
from the mouth of a whale
swimming in a glass of water.

□

**The love of course run did never smooth true.**

## ❧ Trina

Winter has melted into the sea
again
and another unborn spring stirs
within a pregnant ocean
as wave
after wave (after weary)
after wave
extracts its tiny tithe of grain
from grey and jagged rock
and beat, replete—
regreet:
rebeat
and then
again
repeat, and of the waves
that wash away
in whirls of frothing wispy white
which one?
Which one are we?
And grey . . .

And grey is the rock on which we stand,
as grey as the flesh of your once pink hand.
Unto how much grey have we both been damned?
And which of the waves are we?

And grey is the sky where your grey cheek
    blends,
as grey as the haze where the water ends
or continues grey where the surface bends.
And one of these waves are we?

They say that every ninth wave . . . .
but who believes?
And how many bother to count?

Behind your salt-sprayed ear, my lips
bite quiet words.
And then my cold wet nose
touches a delicious chill
that skids its shivering way
across shocked flesh
subsiding where my arms press
stretching warm around
to cup a breast
above each lightly touching palm.
Content.
Content is not enough,—
count.
What, count?
Is there time to believe?
And all those others,
so hard to tell apart,
how much contentment?
Are they searching, too?
For what!
and yet we must
that much we know
we must
deeper than the mirrored blackness
where the backwash water pool
oozes off the rocks
and far beyond the furthest fragile splash of spray.

□

For all too few years in the '50's, a very fortunate few students enjoyed the privilege of an unparalleled educational opportunity. Judson Butler's theories of correlated education coalesced in a two year course at Boston University's College of General Education.

The core curriculum was taught so that all subjects related to each other. When we were being taught something in one course, we were learning its different applications in other disciplines. What we learned in one class might easily show up on a test in one of the others. Everything related to everything else.

At our first gathering in the auditorium, we were told to look to our left and right, because at the end of the two years only one of us would still be there. They weren't kidding. The classes were intense and challenging, and they were exciting. We were given more syllabi and reference material than we could ever assimilate and the amount of homework assigned demanded a minimum of six hours a day, even from the fastest students.

In spite of the grind, the *esprit de corps* was virtually tangible. In addition to determination, an essential ingredient of our survival was a sense of humor.

## ❧ The Birch Society

When looking for veracity
They'll offer you loquacity
To cover their mendacity
And worse, their tongues are acidy
The Birch Society

CHORUS: Our country nurtures
The good John Birchers
The very bottom
Of the Backbone
Of the Great Society

The need for their verbosity
Lies in their false precocity
So fraught with nebulosity
And rife anfractuosity
The Birch Society

CHORUS: Our country nurtures
The good John Birchers
The very bottom
Of the Backbone
Of the Great Society

They brag of their simplicity
And flood you with felicity
To cover their duplicity
While plotting their mendicity
The Birch Society

CHORUS: Our country nurtures
The good John Birchers
The very bottom
Of the Backbone
Of the Great Society

□

The term "modern Renaissance man" used to bother me when I'd see it in print applied to me. In retrospect, though, I suspect that this spirit of the Renaissance was such that it was perfectly natural to be creative in many different fields. The urge to create remains constant: the joy of discovery, experiment, finding solutions, and most especially, of course, the exquisite joy of the finished product when it all works.

Moving from one discipline to another merely means learning how to use a different set of tools. Whether acting, painting, writing, sculpting, composing, or directing, the impulse remains the same. Only the means of achievement vary. What is difficult to say in one discipline may be much more easily expressed in another, or expressed in a completely different way as, for example, depicting dawn in words or paint or music.

My first job after college was as a fledgling announcer for the Concert Network working at a remote FM station on Jerimoth Hill, the highest point in western Rhode Island, so remote that it was five days before the photographer from the Providence paper showed up. By that time the winter sun had changed Beethoven from robust to gaunt.

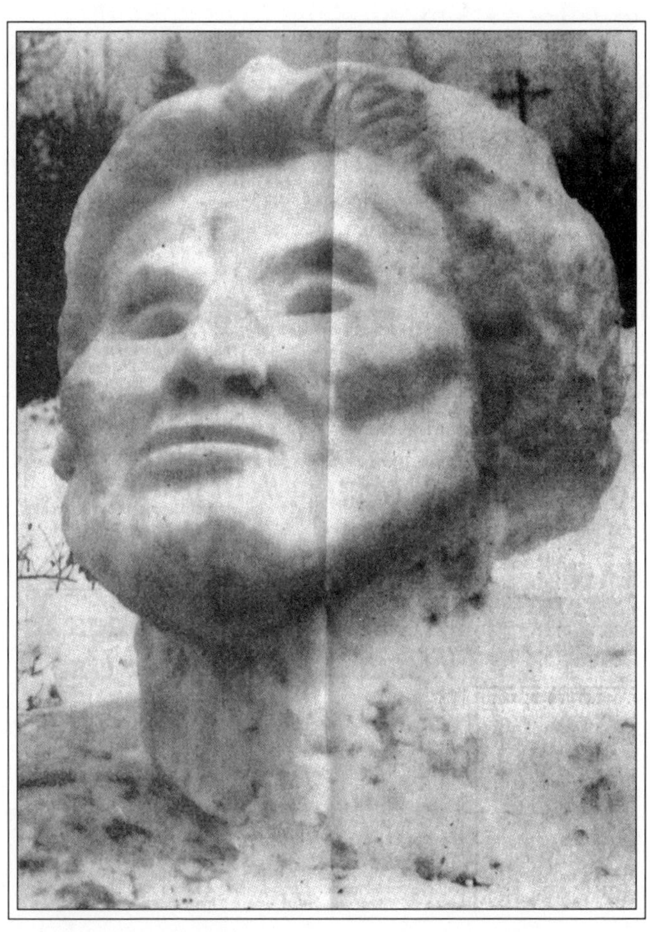

**Shades of Peanuts!** Not to be outdone by the Peanuts cartoon character who keeps a bust of Beethoven on his toy piano, Robert J. Lurtsema, of 3 Douglas Avenue, Providence, took advantage of the snowfall which marooned him temporarily in Foster last week to turn out a work of snow sculpture of the composer. Mr. Lurtsema is an announcing engineer for an FM classical music station and a classical music enthusiast. He took five hours to complete the head.

One of the delights of writing poetry or, for that matter, working in any art form, is that you get to make up the rules as you go along. Not that there aren't already established rules to begin with, and not that you shouldn't learn them. By definition, I think, you can't break rules until you know what they are. Laws maybe, but not rules. Anyway that's not what I'm talking about.

Creative invention is different from learning or breaking rules. It's looking for, and finding forms on your own. Most likely they've been found before. But that doesn't lessen the satisfaction of the discovery. Nor does the probability that they are not new diminish the ardor of the pursuit.

Every verse has its own special challenge. It also tends to dictate its own form. A limerick forced into sonnet form will most likely read like a limerick forced into sonnet form. But that's not what I'm talking about, either. I'm talking about how the form becomes established by the material itself as you go along.

In my early experiments with verse, I found that even rhyme was not necessarily a prerequisite.

## ❧ Lonely

There was a moon
but there wasn't
any you
and I
was lonely
wanting you
walking
with heavy feet
kicking
ahead of me
a purple shadow
in the snow
that looked as lonely
almost completely out of mind
as the world,
so cold and far behind
that solitary
row of footprints,
would have had to be
without you.

Somewhere out there
beyond the black
ungainly mirror
of my mood
there is a time
and as I live
for then
I am alive for then
alive for love
and loving you
my life.

□

When writing verse, it *may* help to know a little bit about metre. It's not a prerequisite but it could help. Speech has a natural rhythm made up of stressed and unstressed syllables. Some words can even change meaning depending on which syllable is stressed, words such as *detail*, *insult*, *research* and *import*, for example.

When words are organized so that the stressed and unstressed syllables fall into a pattern, they can be analyzed. In poetry that process is called *scanning*. Stressed or elongated syllables are indicated by a macron (¯) and the shorter unstressed syllables by a breve (˘). There are four basic metres.

*Iambic* has one short syllable followed by a long: (˘¯).

> When one | attempts | to write | some verse
> It's some- | times bet- | ter, some- | times worse.

*Trochaic* has a macron followed by a breve: (¯˘).

> Writing | verse is | often | easy
> If the | style is | light and | breezy.

*Anapestic* has two short syllables followed by a long: (˘˘¯).

> When the po- | etry's hard | and the writ- | ing gets tough
> Then it's time | to admit | that it might | be enough.

*Dactylic* has a stressed syllable followed by two unstressed ones: (¯˘˘).

> Poetry | dictates its | own kind of | melody
> Working the | syllables | into a | rhapsody.

Each recurrence of a basic metric unit is called a foot. One foot per line is monometer; two feet per line is dimeter; three feet, trimeter. Four feet is tetrameter. The preceding examples of iambic, trochaic, anapestic, and dactylic are all in tetrameter, four stressed syllables per line. Five feet per line is pentameter; six feet, hexameter. Poetry rarely goes beyond this but when it does it's called heptameter for seven feet, octameter for eight and so on.

At this point, it's probably a good idea to stress that you don't need to know any of this to write poetry that scans well. Basically all you need is a feel for the rhythm of speech. Scanning is a tool and tools are there to help make getting the job done a little easier.

There are more metres than the four basic ones cited before.

*Spondee* has two stressed syllables: (––) It was an important variant in Greek and Latin poetry. It is especially valuable in English poetry for emphasis.

Stōp! Wāit!

Some of the less commonly used metres include *Pyrrhic*, two unstressed syllables (˘˘); *Tribrach*, three unstressed syllables (˘˘˘); *Amphibrach*, two short syllables with a long in between (˘–˘); and *Cretic*, two long syllables with a short in between (–˘–).

Combining two or more different metres can be very effective. The following example is a combination of Pyrrhic and Trochaic.

˘ ˘ – ˘ ˘ ˘ – ˘
When we're | waiting | for the | winter
˘ ˘ – ˘ ˘ ˘ – ˘
through the | chilli- | ness of | Autumn
˘ ˘ – ˘ ˘ ˘ – ˘
and the | splendor | of the | summer
˘ ˘ – ˘ ˘ ˘ –
seems so | very | far a- | way.

The choice of the right metre can serve to depict or enhance the subject matter. Dactyls, for example, have a natural galloping rhythm. In the following example the pause at the comma serves as an unaccented beat, an unvoiced syllable that helps to avoid monotony. It generally is a good idea to break up the rhythm every once in a while, but the material itself will probably dictate that anyway.

– ˘ ˘ – ˘ ˘ – ˘ ˘ – ˘
Galloping | rapidly | into the | valley

˘ – ˘ ˘ – ˘ ˘
the | thundering | horses,

– ˘ ˘ – ˘
snorting and | panting

˘ – ˘ ˘ –
were | headed for | home.

Verse does not need rhyme. Blank verse gets along very well without it. So does free verse. Blank verse usually has five iambic feet per line, while free verse is poetry that follows no metric, rhyming or stanzaic form. When there is rhyme it may fall into or be worked into a pattern, called a rhyme scheme.

The most common rhyme schemes are AABBCCDD and ABABCDCD. There can be great pleasure in fashioning or discovering inner rhymes, those that appear within a line. The degree of possible complexity of a rhyme scheme is determined only by the limits of the mind that creates it.

The rhyme scheme of the following is ABACBDCD.

## ❧ Devil

Inside my soul a devil stirs
which fain would raise its head
in spite of how my heart demurs
in spite of how my mind appeals
to keep it trapped inside, instead
the thing will out and show its face
and in the void there steals
remorse to take its place.

□

One of my favorite kind of doodles it the one line drawing. Once the pen touches the paper it stays in continuous motion and is not lifted off the page until the doodle is finished.

The following verse in iambic dimeter has a different kind of rhyme scheme. There are no rhymes within the stanza, but every line rhymes with its counterpart in the other verse.

## ❧ Parting

did I forget
to say goodbye
or is it just
that when you're gone
the gap that's left
is so much greater than
that small forgotten
word of parting
and so much less
than all the things
I might have said
if I had taken time
to abstract
everything
you mean to me

how could I let
the time go by
with childlike trust
in each new dawn—
and then, bereft
of you, have made no plan
nor even sought an
ideal starting
for that caress
that ever sings
inside my head
a tender touch of rhyme
a love tract
that would sting
eternity.

□

Another example of cross verse rhyme is found in the following, where the first five verses rhyme with the last five. The first verse is cross rhymed with the sixth verse, the second with the seventh, and so on.

## ❧ Rain

across town
over the river
and lost
a quick call
then back again
and right on track

a crash
of thunder
and shrouds
of wet grey
swirled by
along the river

lightning
that burst
again
outlining
rock and tree
eerily lighted

a burst
of weather
soaking
the glades
the earth
careening

and yet
with rain
the air
the wood
smelled fresh
and bright

still down
as if forever
storm tossed
the heavy fall
of summer rain
and thunder crack

a flash
from under
the clouds
a jagged spray
and I
felt you shiver

frightening
at first
and then
reclining
next to me
your fear subsided

our first
together
joking
with shades
of mirth
and meaning

so wet
your mane
of hair
so good
your flesh
the night.

□

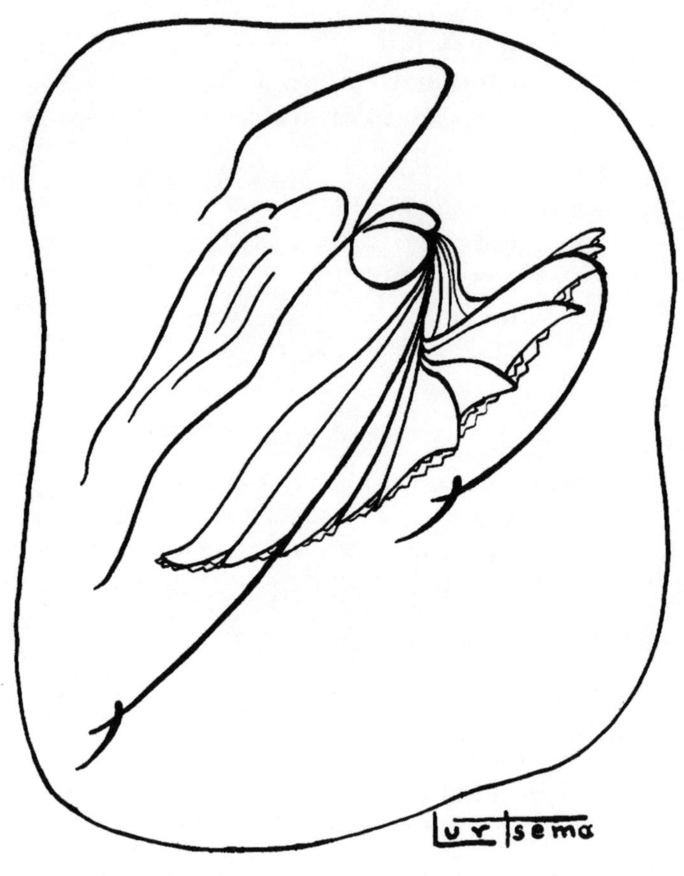
Lurtsema

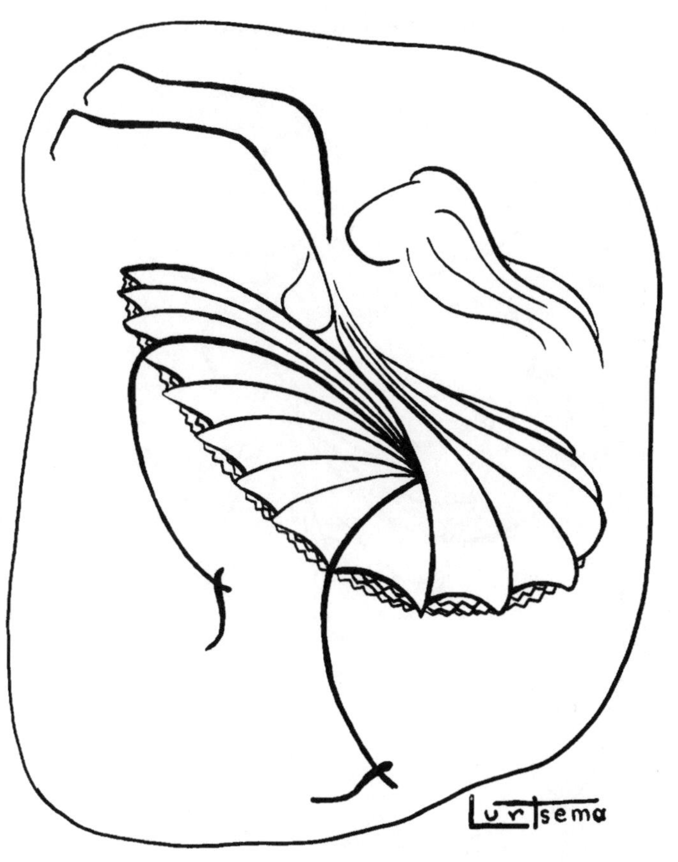
Lurtsema

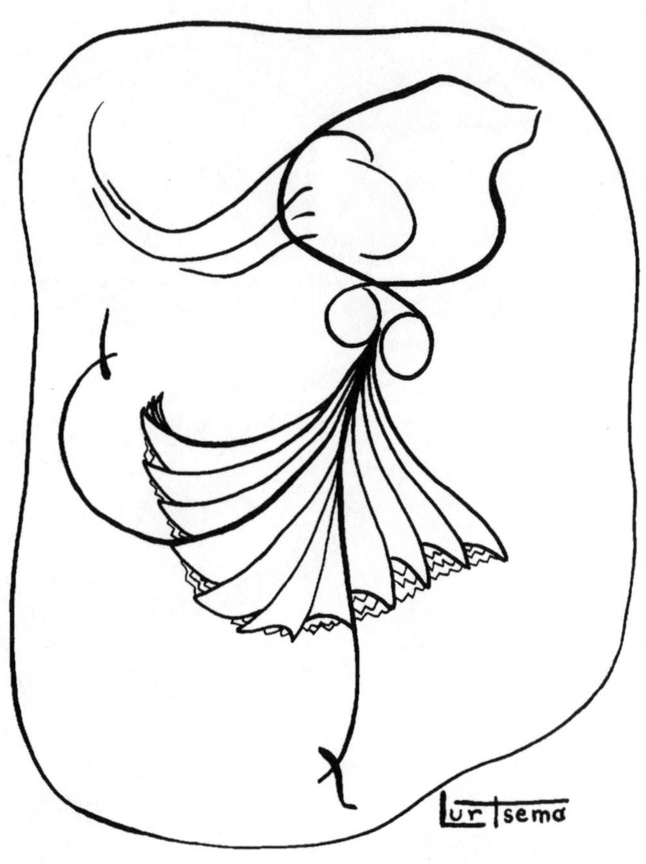
Lurtsema

Sometimes I think of the Muse as an unpredictable Dominatrix. You never know when she'll arrive and you can't depend on her being there when you need her. Once she does show up, she takes charge. You submit, and she has her way with you. Resist, and you're shut off.

She's coy. She plays games with your mind. One minute she's there, leading you on, promising fulfillment, and then, as soon as you start reaching, she's gone. But when she has control and you go along with her, your mind, your whole being gets caught up in the passion of the moment.

Most of the time, I have no idea how a poem I'm writing is going to evolve. The creative process is different than it is in painting or sculpture or even writing music, where you usually proceed step by logical step toward something you can see in your mind or hear in your head. Poetry is more improvisatory, more unpredictable.

A line or phrase that seems to be completely unrelated may pop into your head and end up being the first line or the last except that you couldn't recognize it because you didn't have enough of the other lines to put it with. Or you might end up with the poem all written and find the line left over, unused, only to discover later that it really belongs in another poem you hadn't started writing yet. This, of course, can lead to all kinds of philosophical discussions on just where the material comes from in the first place.

In the following verse, for example, the first and last quatrains arrived and were written down a piece at a time in random disarray, but had to wait until the nine-line middle stanza was complete before I could sort them out. Even now I'm not sure which verse should be first and which last.

## ❧ New Love

So fragile, so tender
  the day, the wine
The sudden splendor
  of finding you mine.

The warm surprise
  of a winter sun
As lethargy dies
  and sadness is done.
In the depths of your eyes
  the promise of fun
Needs no disguise
  with the tryst begun
  and a lover won.

So fragile, so fleeting
  the day, the time
The sudden greeting
  and finding we rhyme.

□

From the mid-fifties to the time that the folk boom happened in the early sixties, Jazz and Poetry enjoyed a brief period of companionship as a form of popular entertainment. The times were tailored for the combination.

Clubs were seeking an inexpensive agenda that would perk up their appeal and bring back clientele who seemed to be looking for more than just another evening of music. Aspiring poets, eager to express their concerns, were looking for a receptive audience. Too young to be daunted by their inexperience, they tilted at the windmills of their own raw emotions.

As they began to attract a following, they were forced to push the muse ever more severely in a bid for fresh material. Sometimes it was hard to tell whether the musicians or the poets were doing the most improvising, but together they rocked the cradle of the seething sixties.

## ❧ Jazz

This is the sound
of swing and stuff.
It stays with you
in the sun.
But mostly it's meant
for late and dark
after the day's all done
after the time
to relax
has come.
This is the time for jazz.
This is the time for loose
and losing yourself
in beat.
This is the cry
in a wandering age
a wondering cage.
Effete?
This is the time for Jazz
Big Jazz
with a capital J.
Tug at the tendons
of feet
and trample
lethargies
of social must.
Our legacy
is jazz.

□

Lurtsemo

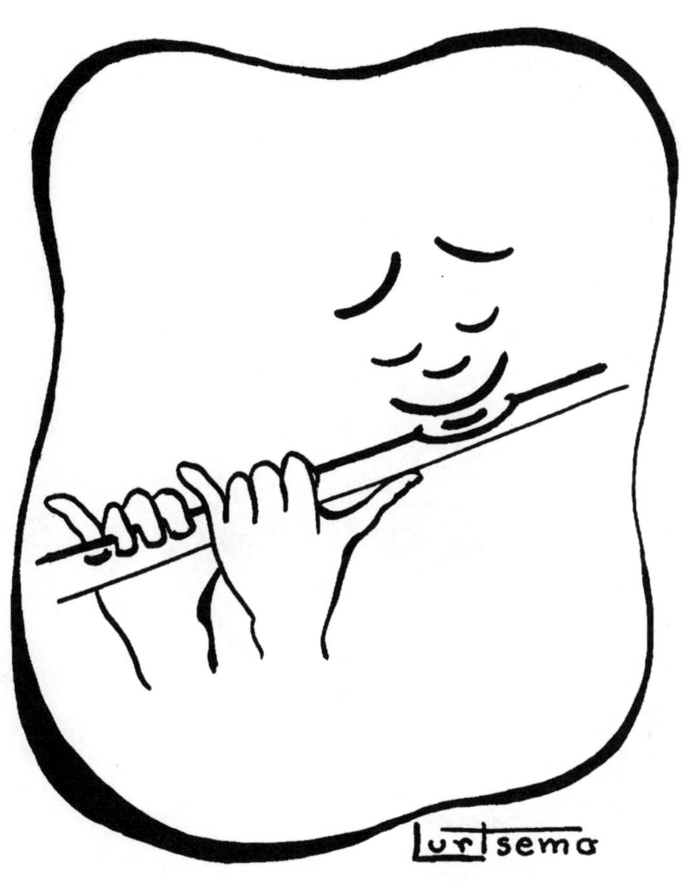
Lurtsema

Kurtsema

Back in the early sixties every new event had a gathering attached to it: opening night parties, press receptions, publisher's previews, art openings, and many more. The mix of people included press and patrons, publishers, promoters, professionals and people who just liked to rub shoulders with people in the arts. There were always of course a few actual artists invited, mostly to add color to the mix.

I was juggling a number of interests at the time: acting, painting, writing, etc., and finding it hard to keep control of all of them. My involvement in so many fields prompted many invitations. Since success in any of my pursuits was dependent on recognition, and on making contacts, I attended many gatherings.

At one of these receptions for artsy types, I was introduced to an attractive redhead who was described to me as an agent. She expressed an interest in my work and asked to see a portfolio. I wasted no time making that happen. She seemed to be impressed and offered to work on my behalf. No contract. No fee. Just a handshake. Symbiosis. It seemed like a great arrangement.

Not long after that, she called, gave me an address, and asked me to meet her there just after dinner. It was an apartment typical of Boston's Back Bay—a living room, bedroom, bath and kitchenette, in a fashionable neighborhood. The resident, a man in his thirties, was the out of town representative for a prestigious New York publication.

She put my portfolio on the coffee table. He skimmed through it quickly, making some favorable comments as he went along. They then went into the other room, for what I assumed was to be a discussion of terms. Wondering what was taking so long, I checked and found that they were not in the bathroom or the kitchenette.

Perhaps it was my daydreaming about what this meeting could lead to that had made me so naive, so slow to catch on to what was really happening, and perhaps I should have hung around to see how things would turn out, but my wounded pride won out.

I never saw him again, but before I left his apartment, I took a blank pad from my portfolio and scribbled the following verse. I made a legible copy, put it on the coffee table, picked up my portfolio and left.

Some months later I ran into her again at an event where she was arguing with her husband, who was pimping for her and complaining that she was holding back on the profits.

# ❧ Swing

Swing from the hip
  for the big time men
for the scene, for the bit
  for back again
till the call comes in
  for the bigger pitch
and the better take.
  For every bitch
  on the make
there's a call
  for all
she can give.

Make the build-up big
  but not too long.
If you're coming on
  well come on strong.
Slide right on in.
  'cause Baby, this life
is all too brief
  and rife
  with grief.
Get yours, Girl, yours.
  Even whores
have got to live.

□

It's funny how one experience can change your whole attitude. "Swing" was written in 1961. Even though I knew it was unreasonable, I never again sought help from an agent after that initial disappointment.

Disappointments, of course, are part of life, and so is learning how to put them aside.

## ❧ Hope

There is a sad
  uncertain time
when parting seems
  the only course
and life makes
  little sense.

But hope, clad
  in jeweled rhyme
provides the
  dreams
  that are the source
of heartache's
  recompense.

□

There are a couple of themes that seem to run through my writing, concepts for which I seem to have a predilection. One is beginnings. Springtime, that glorious beginning when everything is fresh and new and full of hope and promise.

The other is endings which show up with all their attendant sadness in that wrenching time when something that you desperately wish could continue has reached its inevitable end.

Sometimes they happen at the same time.

# ❧ Color

Buds bursting serene
Spring is here, only
Without you it's lonely
  Color it green.

If we hadn't fed
The festival's fire
There'd be no desire
  Color it red.

Mind pictures form
Time cannot dim
Joy to the brim
  Color them warm.

Young memories old
Half open doors
Sanibel's shores
  Color them gold.

When midday is bright
And temper fashions
An hour of passions
  Color them white.

If temerity's slack
Darkness will cover
Timidity, lover
  Color it black.

Games until dawn
A soft disrobing
Of psychic probing
  Color it fawn.

Which of us spoke
The half formed word
Before it was heard
  Color it smoke.

The mind and the hand
Creation's tether
Working together
  Color it grand.

And now without you
A cherished part
Torn from my heart
  Color it blue.

How much of each day
Can we afford
To waste, being bored
  Color it grey.

□

Poetry is difficult to define, maybe even impossible, but it is not difficult to recognize. We can't define masterpieces in music or painting either, but they are clearly discernible. They can be described, but not defined, and even the description is always incomplete.

Not everything that rhymes is verse.

The door-
Bell is ringing
The purple parakeet isn't singing
Any more.

Not all verse is poetry, nor should it be.

Roses are red
But, if violets are blue
Why call them violets?
I don't know. Do you?

An enormous amount of verse is written every year for its utilitarian value, finding its way on to wall hangings, souvenirs, and greeting cards. If you have a knack for rhyme, you can write your own verse on the bottom half of a sheet of paper, fold it over, and draw a little sketch on the outside, *et voilà*, an instant greeting card as personalized as it can be.

It also saves you the cost of a card.

Over the years I must have sent hundreds of greetings, personalized with verse, to friends on special occasions. None of them ever complained of my frugality.

This is one I sent to my long-time friend Russ Clark at the end of 1968. We're still friends.

In the waning days
Of one more year
I can't begin to count
The many ways
I hold you dear
Or gauge the full amount
And as we store
Each happy date
Of this year at its end
I'm thankful for
The turn of fate
That brought me such a friend.

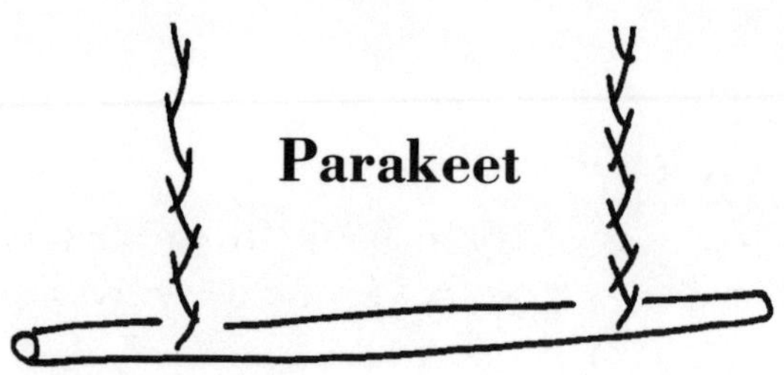

# Parakeet

There's not a thing as absurd
As a parakeet bird
    Who plummets from perches and things
And tumbling down
Like a bumbling clown
    Forgets to rely on his wings!

□

I moved to New York City in 1965. But after trying on the Big Apple for three years, I found it really didn't fit.

Maybe I wasn't being fair. Maybe I never really gave The City a chance. I had hedged my bet and kept my old apartment. Every week for three years I drove back to Boston for my Friday night radio program, Folk City USA on WCRB, spent the weekend and then, late Sunday night or early Monday morning, drove the 210 miles back to work.

## ❧ Manhattan

Canyons of glass,
Stone slabs and steel
Stabbing the street.

Where is the grass
I want to feel
Under my feet?

People who pass
Seem so unreal.

How does one greet
This sorry mass
Lacking in zeal
So incomplete
Impersonal, crass
Who've lost the deal
And won defeat?

And so it was back to Boston, actually to my garret apartment in Cambridge, where I could relax and paint. After the rush and hustle of The City, unscheduled mornings with nothing to do but listen to music and paint were sheer bliss.

I listened to a Boston radio station, WGBH, and a program called "Morning pro musica." It was a high-falutin' snob appeal name that I never would have chosen, but the music was good. I painted seven days a week, which gave me the chance to compare the continuity of the weekday broadcasts when the regular host, Bill Cavness, was there, with the unpredictable, sometimes even chaotic disarray when the program was left to the weekend hosts.

On a busy Saturday morning, early in the summer of 1971, I was painting in my studio with the radio going full blast, which was my usual routine. The familiar voice of Bill Cavness announced a piece by Mozart. "Ah, Mozart," I thought, in happy anticipation. And then came a tiny surprise that was to change my whole life.

It wasn't Mozart, but Enesco. When it became obvious that no correction was being made, I phoned the station. "Bill isn't here," the voice said. "We're running a tape." Actually, it was a tape of only the voice track, which the young board operator, working with a cue sheet, had to play between the records, and he had gotten one piece out of sync. Grateful that I had corrected him before the situation got out of hand, he volunteered the information that Morning pro musica was in need of a part-time weekend host.

I wasn't exactly starving in my garret, but supplies were running low and there were bills to pay. So I got out my ancient Wollensak, and ran off a hasty audition tape, making sure to include titles in half a dozen different languages. I had three different one-page resumés. I wouldn't need the "artist-photographer," or the "actor-director," but armed with the "radio TV" resumé and the audition tape, I showed up at WGBH for an interview, got the job, and started the following weekend. I used records from my own collection, which was more than three times larger, and much more varied than what the station had.

I figured it would be for just three or four months, but a series of events changed my mind. I found I was spending weekdays at the station planning the weekend programs. Bill Cavness opted out of Morning pro musica to devote his energy to Reading Aloud. The station needed a weekday host, and urged me to switch.

I was reluctant to give up the growing weekend audience, and didn't really want a full-time job. But it had become apparent that what the program really needed was the continuity and dependability of a format that was planned and presented by the same person every day. So I countered their proposal with an offer to do the weekdays but not give up the weekends.

They agreed, assuming such an arrangement wouldn't last longer than a month. It did.

I had already established a reputation for breaking the "rules" of broadcasting. Working seven days a week just gave me that much more opportunity. My newscasts, for example, didn't fit the standard mold. I liked to think about what I was saying and I didn't like to feel obliged to rush through it.

For the icy-shower-early-morning-wide-awake types, the slow pace and pauses were excruciating. But for those who were not morning people, and who, like me, preferred to greet the day slowly and quietly, the lack of rat-a-tat was a welcome relief, especially appreciated by those for whom English was a second language.

Normally my first two and a half hours were spent editing the news. Even though the newscasts took up less than 10% of the total broadcast time, I always felt that they were of equal importance to the music. Some days there wouldn't be any news worth reporting, and that's all I would say. At other times an event or topic might merit more time than usual.

The following newscast had its genesis in UPI newswire copy.

## ❧ April

The month of March sped by so fast
That we can still taste February
But now, at last, it's April.
The winds have lost their ferocity
Winter seeps into softening ground
The very air is tense with promise
And all around
Morning has the smell of newness
And the unmistakable awakening of Spring.

Heavy rains wash away the last remains of ice and snow
And rinse the forest clean
Buds long tightly coiled flex and swell
Tiny tips of green break out of earth's confining grip
The matted grass lifts itself off the ground
And trades its yellowed coat for one of brighter green
Hibernating animals shake off their long winter's sleep
Squirrels are practicing their treetop acrobatics
Birds we rarely see are winging northward
And those more familiar are tuning up their mating calls
And tidying up their nest.

April is spring cleaning
Storing away the skis and skates
And heavy winter clothing
Storm windows come down
Lawn chairs and garden hose come out of storage
Along with hammocks, tents
Sleeping bags and picnic gear

Marathoners are training in earnest now
The first ball of the season is thrown
And another pennant race begins
It's time to break out the balls and bats
And racquets and kites
And hunt for the snorkel and fins
Time to get the boat back in the water
Check the barbecue
And see how well the old jalopy
Stood up to the rigors of winter.

April is showers and sunshine
And plowing and planting
Weeding and pruning
And sowing the fields.

It's the magical time of the year
When ladyslippers first appear
As do magnolia and jonquil.

Crocus and forsythia already here
Are joined by tulip, daisy and daffodil.

But the sweet pea, a slender annual vine,
Is the official flower of April
First cultivated in Sicily in 1699.

The April birthstone is the diamond, not a blend
But a single element, found deep within a mine
The hardest substance known,—vital to industry
Treasured by man, and especially by woman.
Crystallized carbon is a girl's best friend.

April is the birthmonth
Of Rachmaninoff and Randall Thompson
Of Emile Zola and Booker T. Washington
Of Andre Previn and Noah Greenberg
Of Charlie Chaplin, Houdini and Audubon
Schnabel, Piatigorsky and Casadesus.

Wilbur Wright was born in April
As were Marconi, Miro and da Vinci
Yehudi Menuhin, Ravi Shankar and Ali Akbar Khan
Queen Isabella, Queen Juliana, Elizabeth II
And Catherine the Great
Prokofiev, Nardini, Tartini and Ginastera
Hans Christian Andersen and Henry James
Paul Robeson, Leonard Warren and Milton Cross
Kathleen Ferrier, Maria Callas and Lily Pons.

Shakespeare and Wordsworth were born in April.
So were Lenin and Hitler
And Jefferson, Monroe and Grant
Barbra Streisand, Ella Fitzgerald and Billie Holiday
Pierre Monteux and Leopold Stokowski
Sir Malcolm Sargent, Sir Thomas Beecham
"Duke" Ellington and the Duke of Wellington.

April is named for Aprilis, a Latin word meaning
"to open."
It is the time of the opening of blossoms,
The opening of streams,
The opening of the earth,
And an open door to summer.

Let us hope,
That we might
Now,
When no place on earth
Is more than moments away
From conflict or communication,
Open our minds to the perils of overpopulation
Open our warehouses to those who hunger
Open our arms to our fellow beings
Open our hearts to understanding
And open our souls to peace.

□

From the very beginning, listener response to Morning pro musica has been gratifying. Not always favorable, but always gratifying. It was a learning experience for me, and it was fun. And it was a joy to hear from listeners who felt the same way.

The audience has always been helpful. Many sensed that I wanted to learn, and were eager to send assistance. Others, appalled by what I did not already know, wrote in to set me straight. I have always felt that criticism was merely a stronger form of suggestion. Had there been no criticism, I would have felt that I was being insufficiently innovative and taking too few chances.

Often listeners would write to me in verse, and when I could, I would show my appreciation by responding in kind. One of the earliest of these, from L. Bancel and Margaret Hockaday La Farge, came from Nantucket.

*30 miles out to sea*
*you come through*
*oh Morning Pro Musica*
*oh you who rise*
*with the dawn*
*now that*
*the laggard sun*
*has caught up to you*
*and chases*
*us to rise in*
*beach plum glow*
*to the voice*
*of you*
*oh Robert J.*
*stay*
*stay*
*we are listening every day*

This was my reply.

*Often I wish*
*that I could be*
*quietly*
*looking out to sea*
*past Nantucket's shore*
*as the sky*
*is blushing*
*at revealing*
*one more*
*stealing*
*day*
*Instead I*
*am rushing*
*with the news*
*button pushing*
*a sham dawn's glow*
*in diode tubes*
*flicker and glitter*
*away*
*another night*
*as transmitter*
*stretches bright*
*antenna arms*
*glistening*
*to the charms*
*of a sun that's real*
*and I am one who can feel*
*some solace*
*in the knowledge*
*that you're listening.*

The future of classical music, in fact of all the arts, is in the education of the young. If we fail to teach, they won't learn. It is always especially gratifying to receive a letter from a youngster, and especially so if it's in verse. The following was written by Maria Barr, age 12, from Dover, New Hampshire.

*Happy Birthday, Robert J.*
*Hearing your show starts Ma's day*

*Missing Lurtsma*
*Hurts Ma-ma.*

*When reception's fuzzy,*
*Ma gets buzzy.*

*Mostly, tho' the signal's clear*
*And Ma's then in good cheer.*

*So please don't let the music stop;*
*(Lotsa times you even please my pop)*

*For more years of music ahead*
*(E'en tho' many composers are dead)*
*We know you'll stand us in good stead*
*Because you use your handsome head.*

*So Happy Birthday again we say*
*As you continue your musical way.*

*From music lovers all around;*
*We want you to know we love*
*your wonderful sound.*

This was my response.

*How kind of you*
*to take the time*
*and trouble too*
*to write a rhyme*
*that's just for me.*

*I was so glad,*
*as you can see,*
*that I just had*
*to set my mind*
*to writing one*
*to you in kind.*

*Besides, it's fun*
*to write in verse*
*and make words rhyme.*

*I could do worse*
*things with my time*
*like waste it, nor*
*could do no less*
*than thank you for*
*your thoughtfulness.*

*I hope this year*
*is great, and brings*
*all kinds of cheer*
*and happy things,*
*with more to come!*

*One last request:*
*please give your mom*
*my very best.*

Johanna C. Sahlin, a listener from New Haven, Connecticut, wrote that during the fund raising drive the audience "was invited to voice criticism and preferences concerning the broadcasting programs. It was suggested that, perhaps, there might be some who object (!) to your voice and may want to hear less of it (!!)"

She included this verse:

*This is a hymn of praise:*
*Robert J. Lurtsema,*
*Morning Pro Musica,*
*Of thee I sing.*

*Others don't like your voice.*
*I think it's wonderful,*
*Never get tired of*
*its raspy ring!*

She also included a column from the book section of the *New York Sunday Times* about "Jiggery-Pokery," a compendium from Atheneum of double dactyls by Anthony Hecht and John Hollander. I sent her the following response.

*Higgledy-piggledy*
*How can I ever say*
*Thank you so much for the*
*Verses you sent.*

*What would I do without*
*Johanna Sahlin and*
*People who offer such*
*Kind sentiment.*

Naturally, any book about double dactyls would capture my interest, this one especially. The double dactyl verse form has very strict rules. There are two verses of four lines each, the first three lines of each verse in dactylic dimetre, with the last line of the first verse rhyming with the last line of the second verse. In addition, the first line is a nonsense line, such as "Higgledy-piggledy"; the second line is a proper name; and at least one of the subsequent lines must be composed of only one word.

This is every bit as complicated as it sounds, but it's still lots of fun. An example quoted in the book is as follows:

*Higgledy-piggledy,*
*Benjamin Harrison,*
*Twenty-third President,*
*Was, and, as such,*

*Served between Clevelands, and*
*Save for this trivial*
*Idiosyncrasy*
*Didn't do much.*

Naturally, I couldn't resist the temptation to try my hand.

*Higgledy-piggledy*
*Robert J. Lurtsema*
*Marching in rhythm with*
*Dactylic feet.*

*One cannot help but to*
*Join the festivities*
*Overemphatically*
*Keeping the beat.*

I generally like doing things chronologically, as with this book, for example. It makes it easier to figure out what should be coming next. The usual format for Morning pro musica is to start with birds at 7:00 (they being the earliest musicians), and then to move through medieval and Renaissance to baroque, rococo, and classic, and from the springboard of the mighty Beethoven through romantic and impressionist to modern. This led one contemporary composer to accuse me of "relegating twentieth century music to the ghetto of the final hour." In spite of his pique, he did have a point.

There are more reasons for following that format than my penchant for temporal symmetry. One is a parallel to the slow-paced newscast for people who ease themselves slowly out of sleep. The familiar harmonies and cadences of early music are much easier to assimilate. If I were to start off with Stockhausen, I might be guilty of causing some innocent listener to stab himself in the eye with his own toothbrush. Another reason is that the earlier music is often of shorter duration, more in keeping with the amount of time listeners have in the early hours.

Contemporary music is often more complex and demands greater concentration from the listener. To put complicated contemporary pieces too early in the day could be doing a disservice to the music, the composer, and the audience. The most compelling reason, however, is that over the years, a vast majority of listeners has stated a preference for that format.

But, if I never varied the format then the early risers would hear only early music, and that would also be a disservice.

So I have always welcomed any pretext to alter the format. Inevitably this has been followed by letters from alarmed listeners fearing that the change might not be temporary. One such foray early in 1983 led a group of listeners to send in a joint letter of protest petitioning a return to early music in the early hours.

I sent this reassurance.

*Dear Sol, Eleanor, Bob, Kathy, Dennis, Ted & Alice . . .*

*Never fear!*
*The excursion*
*as you awoke*
*At the start of the year*
*is but a diversion*
*away from baroque.*

*The early things*
*for which you yearn*
*as the pendulum swings*
*will return.*

Later in 1983 we presented a daily series of the works of Anton Webern commemorating his centenary and ending with a full five hours on the actual anniversary. One of the letters this elicited follows.

*Dear Robert J.,* *12/8/83*

*May I simply extend warm and sincere appreciation for the Webern series, culminating in a marvelous Saturday morning on the 3rd. I think I detected a deeply sympathetic note in your excellent commentary, and you certainly had done your homework! Well, it is magnificent music. Webern was one of the great human beings, as well as a great composer. I am wondering where you managed to find the recording of the Schubert German Dances. Webern mentions that recording in a letter, I think, to Schönberg. And certainly it was a lovely inclusion.*

*Well, perhaps you will do the same for Berg in 1985 (or any time). And an extended Schönberg presentation would be very welcome here, and I imagine in many places.*

*gratefully,*
*Edward Duncan*

On the very same day that I was answering this letter, I received the following:

*December 3, 1983*

*Olé, Robert J.*

*But not for today*
*December très*
*Webern infamé*

*Écrase Boulét*
*Pas Robert J.*

*Had you chosen December 7th for your musical kamikazeing, we would merely have smiled grimly and turned the nob. But we cannot take this lying down. Please postpone Webern, Schoenberg, Hindemith et al until we are well out of bed — say 10. Never play Penderecki. Consider enriching the already sumptuous feast with just a pinch more of Chopin and Liszt, but stay with mostly the Baroque until the 9 o'clock news — at least.*

*We have just moved to Maine, partly so that we may hear your golden voice (and its attendant musical offerings) more clearly. (The rock stations of Long Island add their bit in making that area an impossible one to live in.) We don't want to move again.*

*Your fan of the last 10 years,*

*Clinton W. Trowbridge*

The obvious move was to send Mr. Trowbridge a copy of the letter from Mr. Duncan with the opposing viewpoint, which is what I asked my secretary to do, along with my response, which was as follows:

*Clinton,*

*Please note from the enclosed billet-doux*
*Not everyone agrees with you*
*What destroyed your day made another's complete*
*"One man's poison is another man's meat"*
*One thing I hope you'll be pleased to know*
*It's only every fifty years or so*
*I'm sorry it caused you such agony*
*Don't listen in 2033.*

*Robert J.*

I was unaware that my secretary had failed to enclose Mr. Duncan's letter until I received the following gem:

*Robert J.*

*The billet-doux you forgot to enclose,*
*So I can only assume, or suppose,*
*That some compliment to you was sent*
*About Pendereski or Webern, not a lament.*
*I'm delighted to hear it; it gives me great joy.*
*It's as if I were a father, and it was a boy.*
*'Tis true, one man's meat to another spells gruel,*
*But do not suppose we're made up of all fool.*
*To our voice give an ear, to our taste a small nod;*
*I know in your programming we cannot play God.*
*We plead with you earnestly; shout loud as we can:*
*Nix mit der Pendereski! Up mit Chopin!*

*Clinton W. Trowbridge*

Not long after that, I received another letter on the same subject from a listener in Jaffrey Center, New Hampshire.

*Avid listener wishes a curbing*
*Of all music so new it's disturbing!*
*Around nineteen-ten*
*Something happened, I ken*
*To make music not calm, but perturbing!*

*But what Mozart and Haydn did write,*
*Makes the world and our days start out right!*
*A miraculous feat*
*Melding melody-beat!*
*But this new stuff sounds more like a blight!*

*Perhaps it is good for our souls*
*To have senses raked over the coals*
*But old-fashioned opera*
*Starts day fitting and proper-a*
*Would you note this on listener polls?*

*Patricia G. French*

A three limerick offering warranted a three limerick response:

*Dear Patricia:*

*If listeners say they are fond*
*Of music that goes far beyond*
*A conventional score*
*And they want to hear more,*
*I have only one way to respond.*

*Though it may not have withstood time's test*
*And may not be what we like best,*
*If they bothered to ask,*
*I have my assigned task*
*And honor I must their request.*

*The balance when all's said and done*
*Is certainly not one to one,*
*But much more in favor*
*Of pieces we savor*
*And sometimes new pieces are fun.*

*Robert J.*

A couple of months later, she wrote again, this time on a different subject.

*Dear Robert J.;*

*On May twenty-third, working in study,*
*Some notations on Mozart, I heard*
*Revered name was frequently mentioned*
*But my distance, from source, did too muddy*
*The voices, from whence they occurred.*
*A deadline, (my work is unpensioned)*
*Prevented my fullest attention*
*Being given to words that were said.*
*Thus I fear that my pow'rs for retention*
*Became, temporarily, dead!*
*I wish you might send me a transcript,*
*(From your files- if they're not a sealed crypt.)*
*That I might better know competition*
*And give to him due recognition.*

*Pat French*

Much as I would have liked to have honored her request, all I could do was to send the following reply:

*Dear Patricia:*

*Much though I would like to comply*
*with what seems a simple request,*
*I am sorry to have to reply*
*that even for things deemed the best,*
*there's no way that we could afford*
*to transcribe the day's conversation.*
*Someone would have to record*
*each line, like taking dictation.*
*The funds are just unavailable*
*to pay someone for such tedium.*
*One fact remains unassailable.*
*Radio's an ephemeral medium.*

*Robert J.*

One of the inescapable activities of public broadcasting is fund raising. Often along with the check will be a bit of verse, as in this sample from long-time supporters Katinka and Loring Coleman of Harvard, Massachusetts.

*For Robert J.*
*At break of day—*
*For birdsong matutinal*
*Support enclosed*
*In our small way*
*As thanks and with approval!*

This was my reply.

*Dear Loring & Katinka:*

*It's kind of you*
*to take the time*
*to put your sentiments*
*in rhyme*

*The pleasant things*
*you had to say*
*added sparkle to*
*my day*

*The verse just made*
*them that much better*
*So thank you for*
*your thoughtful letter*

*Robert J.*

Over the years, many listeners, knowing that I made a sincere effort to pronounce names correctly, have been kind enough to send me helpful suggestions. I have openly encouraged this practice, grateful for the opportunity to learn.

Karl V. Teeter, Professor of Linguistics Emeritus at Harvard University, decided I needed to be reminded of one of his earlier suggestions.

*Dear Robert:*

*Some years ago I proved to you that the correct pronunciation of the ambiguously spelled name of John Dowland was in fact Dough-land, pointing out the contemporary assonance shown in the composition Semper Dolens Semper Dowland, where the o of dolens is clearly the long o. At the time you adopted this pronunciation, and I recall your using it for some time. I am surprised, therefore, to hear you this morning reverting to the pronunciation of the ignorant majority. I hope you may reconsider this.*

*Yours,*
*Karl V. Teeter*
*Professor of Linguistics, Emeritus*
*Harvard University*

Even though he hadn't written to me in verse, I felt compelled to respond with the following rhyme:

*Dear Karl:*

*From sheepland down to cowland,*
*From the highlands to the lowlands,*
*All the music of John Dowland*
*Is the same as old John Dowland's*

*It's a topic for debate,*
*How one opts to say the name,*
*What one loves another hates,*
*But the music's still the same.*

Sometimes an even more effective way to respond to a letter is with a quick sketch. It's so much easier to draw a picture than to write 10,000 words.

*Dear Mr. Lurtsema:* *Nov. 13, 1984*

*Thank you very much for your wonderful years with 'Morning Pro Musica'. I am always particularly impressed with the accurate pronunciation you have of particularly difficult foreign names. You clearly went to some trouble to learn how to pronounce the Hungarians and Czechs with the accent always on the first syllable. Therefore, it struck me as strange that in a city of so many Italians, you have stumbled on the Italian 'z' of Donizetti. It is never pronounced like an English 'z'. It is either 'ts' as in 'cats' or 'dz' as in 'adze', doubled: "--t-ts-" or "--d-dz-". (Cf. Ralph Errole, Italian Diction for Singers, 3rd ed., 1963, for a phonetic transcription of this particular composer's name, p. 107) (ts). Also, when you give the correct pronunciation of a particularly recondite language, could you please spell the name? A great admirer, Stephen P. Gross*

Robert J. Lurtsema

My inability to recall all seven deadly sins prompted this letter from Bob Morris of Denmark, Maine:

*Dear RJL:*

*Should you be called upon ever again to list (or live) the Seven Deadly Sins, here's a mnemonic that I used to give to my literature students. It was about the only thing they ever remembered from my courses!*

*WASPLEG*

*I.e., Wrath, Avarice, Sloth, Pride, Lechery, Envy, Gluttony.*

which inspired this response:

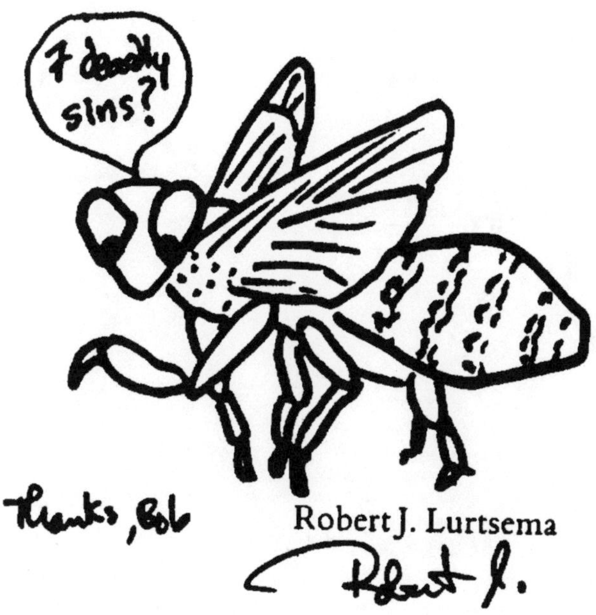

*13th · Feb · 82*

*Dear Mr. Leurtzema*

*I don't want to appear fussy, but I rather think that tankers (cf your broadcast news of this date) have hulls, not hulks. Television has hulks—incredible as that may seem.*

*Faithfully,*
*John and Joanne Douglas*

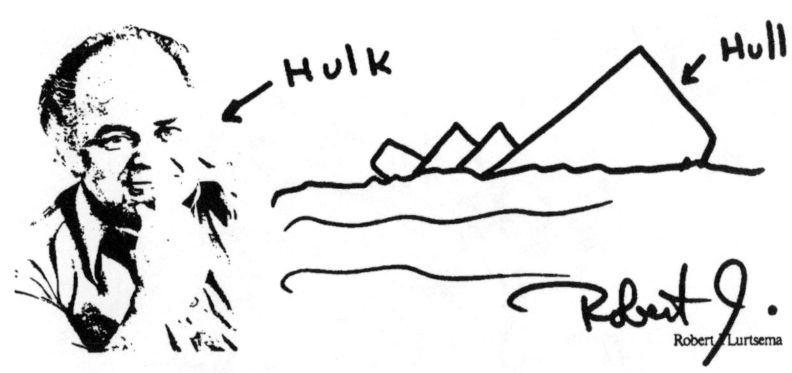

Here's a postcard that arrived in time for the holidays.

*We tried to get through on your phone-in two weeks ago, anent Mr. Lurtsema's program. The lines were constantly busy. We used to be regular listeners but rarely tune in now because the sameness of the music has become boring to us, and Mr. Lurtsema's voice annoys our pig.*

*Sincerely,*

*Raymond Izbicki*
*Stonington, Conn.*

This seemed appropriate.

Sometimes there doesn't seem to be any way to respond to a letter *except* with a drawing, as with this piece of correspondence from Jim Clow of Contoocook, New Hampshire.

Dear RoberT,

You are a boob!

Your show begins with birds AT 7:00!

The birds do NOT, I repeaT, DO NOT, begin singing aT 7:00!

There for I wish you would ANNOUNCE in fronT of The whole, don't get nervous, audience:

"Birds do noT," or rather should I SAY, "Some birds like peanuT butter with Thier Spaghetti."

I Love you.

JIM CLOW

Jim,

Robert

Record jackets come in many different languages. Sometimes, when concentration is divided, translating them can provide the attentive listener with an unexpected chuckle.

*Dear Robert J.* *July 21, 1987*

*On or about July 12 of this year you played a recording of Schubert's "The Shepherd on the Rock" on your program. You announced it as "The Shepherd on the Rocks" which brought a chuckle to me as I am sure to many others. Next time around let's put our poor shepherd on the proper singular footing.*

*Yours truly,*

*Booth Simpson*

June 26, 1991 was my twentieth anniversary as host of Morning pro musica. Listeners have always responded generously with congratulations and encouragement on birthdays, anniversaries, and holidays, and this one was no exception. Some letters needed a specific reply, but I wanted to answer them all. So I took them with me in July to Woodstock, New York, and read through them as I spent a few days enjoying the hospitality of Robert Starer and Gail Godwin. Theirs is such a blockbuster combination of talent that I think the Muse must be a permanent resident. She certainly was right there urging me on.

## ❧ 20th anniVERSary

In June of 1971
I had only just begun
And I assumed that I'd be through
Long before 1972
But the program got the best of me
And soon it was 1973.
I dug in hard in '74
What little I learned made me yearn for more
And so in 1975
I decided to keep the quest alive.
Music and news is a challenging mix
So I studied harder in '76.
'77 slid into '78
And everything was going just great
Improving with age like vintage wine
And we breezed right on through '79.
1980 was no time to quit
Just as we were getting the hang of it.
It was even beginning to feel like fun
And suddenly it was '81.
Since I started ten years had passed
And it had all gone by so fast
I hardly noticed how it flew
And then it was 1982.
Working seven days a week
I'd just begun to hit my peak.
Not that it was all a piece of cake.
There were choices that were hard to make
Some that were mine, some made for me
With which I hardly could agree
Battles I was obliged to fight

When I believed the cause was right
But even though the times got rough
A single decade was not enough.
I was ready for a whole lot more
As '83 rolled into '84.
Challenge was something on which to thrive
And we knew as we flew through '85
What wasn't broken, we didn't need to fix.
That kept us humming through '86.
Time spent working is time well spent.
'87 came and '87 went
And we didn't have very long to wait
Before we'd gone through '88.
There's something about piling year on year
That seems to make them disappear
Something that's very hard to define
But that's what happened to '89
And it seemed that '90 had hardly begun
When all of a sudden it was '91.
Another year was gone, another decade too
And I thought of how much I owe to you.
Whenever things were getting rough
And I was thinking I'd had enough
Somehow it never seemed to fail
I was sure to find in the morning's mail
A description of what a program meant
Some thanks or praise or encouragement
A well chosen card or a thoughtful letter
And times that were hard got so much better
So, thank you friend, for helping me through
As two decades end, there's another that's new.

□

Ophrah Yerushalmi, an Israeli pianist, asked me if I would be interested in appearing with her to narrate a poem called "Lenore." I said, "Sure," and waited for the text to arrive.

It was in German. That wasn't a surprise. She had told me that, and also that she would send along a couple of translations, and I could pick the one I wanted. They *were* a surprise. They were both impossible.

Lenore, a 64-verse poem, was written by Gottfried August Bürger. It was probably the most famous 19th century vehicle for melodeclamation, the art of dramatic reading in public. In an age when there were no movies, no television, no Nintendo, and few vaudeville houses, melodeclamation was the cat's meow.

The two translations were worse than anything the cat dragged in. They were as outdated for today as television was advanced for then. Reading either one in public would have been laughable.

The performance was a little over three months away. So I told Ophrah I would perform, but with my own translation. Fools rush in, etc.

To begin with, I didn't speak German. I didn't understand German. This was long before the two scholarships I was given by the Goethe Institute. But the performance was to be in English, and I did speak that. Also, I had many German-speaking friends. Lisa Lisco, a volunteer at the station, wrote the first transliteration for me and others followed. I got the best German dictionary I could and worked every night for three months.

Franz Liszt had set the poem to music, and I was convinced that a performing translation had to keep the exact metre and rhyme scheme as the original, without adding anything to or taking anything away from the text. Searching for the exact word become a major preoccupation. Even my producer, Leslie Warshaw, who was most often able to come up with the word I sought, was driven to the limits of her patience.

Finally, it was finished. The first of many performances was in the courtyard of Harvard University's Fogg Art Museum. I always wanted to publish the German and English texts side by side. Here they are.

## ❧ Lenore

Lenore fuhr ums Morgenrot
Empor aus schweren Träumen:
„Bist untreu, Wilhelm, oder tot?
Wie lange willst du säumen?“—

Er war mit König Friedrichs Macht
Gezogen in die Prager Schlacht
Und hatte nicht geschrieben,
Ob er gesund geblieben.

Der König und die Kaiserin,
Des langen Haders müde,
Erweichten ihren harten Sinn
Und machten endlich Friede;

Und jedes Heer, mit Sing und Sang,
Mit Paukenschlag und Kling und Klang,
Geschmückt mit grünen Reisern,
Zog heim zu seinen Häusern.

Und überall, allüberall
Auf Wegen und auf Stegen,
Zog alt und jung dem Jubelschall
Der Kommenden entgegen.

Gottlob! rief Kind und Gattin laut,
Willkommen! manche frohe Braut.
Ach! aber für Lenoren
War Gruß und Kuß verloren.

## ❧ Lenore

At dawn, Lenore rose up in bed
Her dreams with omens smitten.
"Are you untrue, William, or dead?
So long since you have written."

He with King Frederick's men had found,
At Prague, the bloodied battleground;
But sent her not one letter
If he fared ill or better.

The Empress and the King, by chance
Had wearied of defiance,
Softened their former warlike stance
And formed a long alliance.

And so the troops, with shouts and yells,
With songs and cheers, with drums and bells,
Green laurels on their blouses,
Came home to their own houses.

And everywhere along the way
On roads and paths for miles
Merged old and young with loud "Hurray"
Through joyful tears and smiles.

"Praise God," the wives and children cried.
"Oh, welcome back" the young brides sighed.
But for Lenore, no greeting.
No kiss, no happy meeting.

Sie frug den Zug wohl auf und ab
Und frug nach allen Namen;
Doch keiner war, der Kundschaft gab,
Von allen, so da kamen.

Als nun das Heer vorüber war,
Zerraufte sie ihr Rabenhaar
Und warf sich hin zur Erde
Mit wütiger Gebärde.

Die Mutter lief wohl hin zu ihr:—
„Ach, daß sich Gott erbarme!
Du trautes Kind, was ist mit dir?“—
Und schloß sie in die Arme.—

„O Mutter, Mutter! hin ist hin!
Nun fahre Welt und alles hin!
Bei Gott ist kein Erbarmen.
O weh, o weh mir Armen!“—

„Hilf Gott, hilf! Sieh uns gnädig an!
Kind, bet ein Vaterunser!
Was Gott tut, das ist wohlgetan.
Gott, Gott erbarmt sich unser!“—

„O Mutter, Mutter! Eitler Wahn!
Gott hat an mir nicht wohlgetan!
Was half, was half mein Beten?
Nun ist's nicht mehr vonnöten.“—

„Hilf Gott, hilf! Wer den Vater kennt,
Der weiß, er hilft den Kindern.
Das hochgelobte Sakrament
Wird deinen Jammer lindern.“—

She ran to each and asked his name
with mounting desperation,
But not one man of those who came
Could give her information.

And when the troops had left her there
She wept and tore her raven hair;
Upon the ground she rolled
With gestures uncontrolled.

Her mother rushed up to her side
"Oh Lord, with mercy mild,"
She took her in her arms and cried,
"Have mercy on my child!"

"Oh Mother, Mother, gone is gone.
I care not if the world goes on.
God's mercy is denied me
And anguish claws inside me."

"Help, Lord, help! Oh merciful One.
Kneel, my child, and pray,
For what God does is rightly done
And prayer's the only way."

"Oh Mother, Mother, can't you see
That God has not done right by me?
What sense is there in prayers
When God no longer cares?"

"Help, Lord, help! Those who believe
In Him need never languish.
The blessed sacrament receive
And that will soothe your anguish."

„O Mutter, Mutter! was mich brennt,
Das lindert mir kein Sakrament!
Kein Sakrament mag Leben
Den Toten wiedergeben."—

„Hör, Kind! wie, wenn der falsche Mann
Im fernen Ungerlande
Sich seines Glaubens abgetan
Zum neuen Ehebande?

Laß fahren, Kind, sein Herz dahin!
Er hat es nimmermehr Gewinn!
Wann Seel' und Leib sich trennen,
Wird ihn sein Meineid brennen."—

„O Mutter, Mutter! Hin ist hin!
Verloren ist verloren!
Der Tod, der Tod ist mein Gewinn!
O wär' ich nie geboren!

Lösch aus, mein Licht, auf ewig aus!
Stirb hin, stirb hin in Nacht und Graus!
Bei Gott ist kein Erbarmen.
O weh, o weh mir Armen!"—

„Hilf Gott, hilf! Geh nicht ins Gericht
Mit deinem armen Kinde!
Sie weiß nicht, was die Zunge spricht.
Behalt ihr nicht die Sünde!

Ach, Kind, vergiß dein irdisch Leid
Und denk an Gott und Seligkeit!
So wird doch deiner Seelen
Der Bräutigam nicht fehlen."—

"Oh Mother, Mother, the pain inside
No ritual can turn aside;
No sacrament restore
The dead to life once more."

"Listen, Daughter, he may have strayed,
In distant lands despairing,
Forgot the promises he made
And sought another's sharing.

Relent, my child, let his heart go.
He is not worth the grief you show.
When soul and body fail
He'll burn for his betrayal."

"Oh, Mother, Mother, gone is gone.
Forlorn remains forlorn.
Death is my wish. I can't go on.
I wish I'd not been born.

Go out, my light, forever out.
Die, when night is endless doubt.
God's mercy is denied me
And anguish claws inside me."

"Help, Lord, help! Judge not your child.
She knows not what she's saying.
It's just her tongue that so reviled.
Please overlook her straying.

Ah, Child, forget your earthly cares
And turn your thoughts again to prayers.
Thus will your soul recover
And no more miss your lover."

„O Mutter! Was ist Seligkeit?
O Mutter! Was ist Hölle?
Bei ihm, bei ihm ist Seligkeit,
Und ohne Wilhelm Hölle!—

Lösch aus, mein Licht, auf ewig aus!
Stirb hin, stirb hin in Nacht und Graus!
Ohn' ihn mag ich auf Erden,
Mag dort nicht selig werden."— — —

So wütete Verzweifelung
Ihr in Gehirn und Adern,
Sie fuhr mit Gottes Vorsehung
Vermessen fort zu hadern;

Zerschlug den Busen und zerrang
Die Hand bis Sonnenuntergang,
Bis auf am Himmelsbogen
Die goldnen Sterne zogen.

Und außen, horch! ging's trapp trapp trapp,
Als wie von Rosseshufen;
Und klirrend stieg ein Reiter ab
An des Geländers Stufen;

Und horch! und horch! den Pfortenring
Ganz lose, leise, klinglingling!
Dann kamen durch die Pforte
Vernehmlich diese Worte:

„Holla, Holla! Tu auf, mein Kind!
Schläfst, Liebchen, oder wachst du?
Wie bist noch gegen mich gesinnt?
Und weinest oder lachst du?"—

"Oh Mother, Mother, what is happiness?
Oh Mother, what is Hell?
With William, that's my happiness
And without him, that is Hell.

Go out, my light, forever out.
Die, when night is endless doubt.
For me there is no mirth
Without him on this earth."

Thus raged on thru her brain and veins
Despair's contamination.
She fought the will that God ordains
With bold determination.

She beat her breast and wrung her hands
Until the sunset flushed the lands,
Until thru night's domed lining
The golden stars were shining.

And outside. Listen! Trepp, trepp, trepp,
A horse's hooves came pounding.
Dismounting by the outside step,
The clink of armor sounding.

And hush! Now, hush! The doorbell rings
So soft and quietly it sings.
And then the quiet broken
By words distinctly spoken.

"Hello, Love. Open up the door.
Are you awake or sleeping?
What are your thoughts of me, Lenore?
Are you laughing, Child, or weeping?"

„Ach, Wilhelm, du?—So spät bei Nacht?—
Geweinet hab ich und gewacht;
Ach, großes Leid erlitten!
Wo kommst du hergeritten?"—

„Wir satteln nur um Mitternacht.
Weit ritt ich her von Böhmen.
Ich habe spät mich aufgemacht
Und will dich mit mir nehmen."—

„Ach, Wilhelm, erst herein geschwind!
Den Hagedorn durchsaust der Wind,
Herein, in meinen Armen,
Herzliebster, zu erwarmen!"—

„Laß sausen durch den Hagedorn,
Laß sausen, Kind, laß sausen!
Der Rappe scharrt; es klirrt der Sporn,
Ich darf allhier nicht hausen.

Komm, schürze, spring und schwinge dich
Auf meinen Rappen hinter mich!
Muß heut noch hundert Meilen
Mit dir ins Brautbett eilen."

„Ach! wolltest hundert Meilen noch
Mich heut ins Brautbett tragen?
Und horch! es brummt die Glocke noch,
Die elf schon angeschlagen."—

„Sieh hin, sieh her! der Mond scheint hell.
Wir und die Toten reiten schnell.
Ich bringe dich, zur Wette,
Noch heut ins Hochzeitsbette."—

"Ah, William, you! So late at night?
Such grief and vigil were my plight,
For I had heard no tiding.
From where do you come riding?"

"We saddled up past midnight's chime
In far Bohemia's bourn,
And now there is but little time,
With me you must return."

"Ah, William, first come quickly in.
The hawthorn's chilled by bitter wind.
Here in my arms discover
The warmth saved for my lover."

"Let the wind blow thru the hawthorn's burrs,
Let it continue blowing.
The pawing horse and clattering spurs
Compel us to be going.

Come, Child, get dressed. I know our course.
Spring up behind me on my horse.
A hundred miles ahead
We'll share our bridal bed."

"Oh, must we cover so much ground
To reach our bed of pleasure?
For listen, where the bells still sound
Eleven hours measure."

"Look there, Child, how the moon shines bright.
We, and the Dead, ride fast tonight.
Before this day has fled
We'll reach our bridal bed."

„Sag an, wo ist dein Kämmerlein?
Wo? Wie dein Hochzeitsbettchen?"—
„Weit, weit von hier!—Still, kühl und klein!—
Sechs Bretter und zwei Brettchen!"—

„Hat's Raum für mich?"—„Für dich und mich!
Komm, schürze, spring und schwinge dich!
Die Hochzeitsgäste hoffen;
Die Kammer steht uns offen."—

Schön Liebchen schürzte, sprang und schwang
Sich auf das Roß behende;
Wohl um den trauten Reiter schlang
Sie ihre Lilienhände;

Und hurre hurre, hop hop hop!
Ging's fort in sausendem Galopp,
Daß Roß und Reiter schnoben
Und Kies und Funken stoben.

Zur rechten und zur linken Hand,
Vorbei vor ihren Blicken,
Wie flogen Anger, Heid' und Land!
Wie donnerten die Brücken!—

„Graut Liebchen auch?—Der Mond scheint hell!
Hurra! die Toten reiten schnell!
Graut Liebchen auch vor Toten?"—
„Ach nein!—Doch laß die Toten!"—

Was klang dort für Gesang und Klang?
Was flatterten die Raben?—
Horch, Glockenklang! horch, Totensang:
„Laßt uns den Leib begraben!"

"Tell me, where is your chamber hall?
And the bridal bed, what sort?"
"Far, far from here, calm, cool and small.
Six long planks, and two short."

"There's room for me?" "For you and me!
Come dress! Jump on, and you will see.
Our guests are celebrating.
Our chamber's open, waiting."

The lovely maiden dressed in haste,
Sprang up, for she was agile,
And hugged around her lover's waist
Her hands so white and fragile.

And rapidly, yard after yard,
Both horse and rider breathing hard,
Increased their pace of travel
As hooves struck sparks from gravel.

And on the left, and on the right,
Their eyes were full of wonder,
As heath and meadow flew from sight
And bridges boomed with thunder.

"Afraid, my love? The moon shines bright.
Hurrah! The Dead ride fast tonight.
Is Death so terrifying?"
"Ah, no! Don't speak of dying."

What sound came then of tolling bells?
What flapping wings of ravens?
As song of Death in chorus swells,
Let's grant the Dead their havens."

Und näher zog ein Leichenzug,
Der Sarg und Totenbahre trug.
Das Lied war zu vergleichen
Dem Unkenruf in Teichen.

„Nach Mitternacht begrabt den Leib
Mit Klang und Sang und Klage!
Jetzt führ ich heim mein junges Weib.
Mit, mit zum Brautgelage!

Komm, Küster, hier! Komm mit dem Chor,
Und gurgle mir das Brautlied vor!
Komm, Pfaff', und sprich den Segen,
Eh' wir zu Bett uns legen!"—

Still Klang und Sang.—Die Bahre schwand.—
Gehorsam seinem Rufen
Kam's, hurre hurre! nachgerannt,
Hart hinter's Rappen Hufen.

Und immer weiter, hop hop hop!
Ging's fort in sausendem Galopp,
Daß Roß und Reiter schnoben,
Und Kies und Funken stoben.

Wie flogen rechts, wie flogen links
Gebirge, Bäum' und Hecken!
Wie flogen links und rechts und links
Die Dörfer, Städt' und Flecken!—

„Graut Liebchen auch?—Der Mond scheint hell!
Hurra! die Toten reiten schnell!
Graut Liebchen auch vor Toten?"—
„Ach! Laß sie ruhn, die Toten!"—

A funeral cortege drew near
With coffin high upon its bier.
The dirge they croaked was harsh as
The bullfrogs in the marshes.

"Tonight your dead you bury there
With dirges, bells and chorus.
But I, my young bride take to where
The bridal feast waits for us.

Come, Sacristan, come with your choir.
Let's hear the bridal song. And, Friar,
We'll hear the blessing said
Before we lie in bed."

The bells grew still. So did the song
Obediently mind him.
And hurriedly the ghostly throng
Then followed close behind him.

And ever further on they fled,
The galloping horse and rider sped,
Increased their pace of travel
As hooves struck sparks from gravel.

And on the left and right flew past
The mountains, lakes and ledges.
On right and left flew by so fast
The towns and trees and hedges.

"Afraid, my love? The moon shines bright.
Hurrah! The Dead ride fast tonight.
Is Death so terrifying?"
"Ah, let them rest, the dying."

Sieh da! sieh da! am Hochgericht
Tanzt um des Rades Spindel,
Halb sichtbarlich bei Mondenlicht,
Ein luftiges Gesindel.—

„Sasa! Gesindel, hier! Komm hier!
Gesindel, komm und folge mir!
Tanz uns den Hochzeitreigen,
Wann wir zu Bette steigen!"—

Und das Gesindel, husch husch husch!
Kam hinten nachgeprasselt,
Wie Wirbelwind am Haselbusch
Durch dürre Blätter rasselt.

Und weiter, weiter, hop hop hop!
Ging's fort in sausendem Galopp,
Daß Roß und Reiter schnoben,
Und Kies und Funken stoben.

Wie flog, was rund der Mond beschien,
Wie flog es in die Ferne!
Wie flogen oben überhin
Der Himmel und die Sterne!—

„Graut Liebchen auch?—Der Mond scheint hell!
Hurra! die Toten reiten schnell!
Graut Liebchen auch vor Toten?"—
„O weh! Laß ruhn die Toten!"— — —

„Rapp'! Rapp'! Mich dünkt, der Hahn schon ruft.—
Bald wird der Sand verrinnen—
Rapp'! Rapp'! Ich wittre Morgenluft—
Rapp'! Tummle dich von hinnen!—

Look there! Look! At the gallows tree
On the wheel's spindle dancing.
Half visibly, by moonlight see
An airy horde advancing.

"Ho, Rabble, here! Come over here!
Come, Rabble, come! And follow near.
A wedding dance we'll need
When we to bed proceed."

The rabble, with an eerie whoosh
Fell in behind them, prattling
Like whirlwinds thru the hazel bush,
Like wind thru dry leaves rattling.

And further, further on they fled,
The galloping horse and rider sped,
Increased their pace of travel
As hooves struck sparks from gravel.

How rapidly the moonlit view
Rushed past into the distance.
The earth, the stars and heavens flew,
Urged on by speed's insistence.

"Afraid, my love? The moon shines bright.
Hurrah! The Dead ride fast tonight.
Is Death still terrifying?"
"Alas! Don't speak of dying."

"On, Horse! I think the rooster crows.
The sands run out, I fear.
On, Horse! The east is tinged with rose.
My horse, make haste from here.

Vollbracht, vollbracht ist unser Lauf!
Das Hochzeitsbette tut sich auf!
Die Toten reiten schnelle!
Wir sind, wir sind zur Stelle."— — —

Rasch auf ein eisern Gittertor
Ging's mit verhängtem Zügel.
Mit schwanker Gert' ein Schlag davor
Zersprengte Schloß und Riegel.

Die Flügel flogen klirrend auf,
Und über Gräber ging der Lauf.
Es blinkten Leichensteine
Rundum im Mondenscheine.

Ha sieh! Ha sieh! im Augenblick,
Huhu! ein gräßlich Wunder!
Des Reiters Koller, Stück für Stück,
Fiel ab wie mürber Zunder,

Zum Schädel, ohne Zopf und Schopf,
Zum nackten Schädel ward sein Kopf;
Sein Körper zum Gerippe,
Mit Stundenglas und Hippe.

Hoch bäumte sich, wild schnob der Rapp',
Und sprühte Feuerfunken;
Und hui! war's unter ihr hinab
Verschwunden und versunken.

Geheul! Geheul aus hoher Luft,
Gewinsel kam aus tiefer Gruft.
Lenorens Herz, mit Beben,
Rang zwischen Tod und Leben.

At last! The ending of our ride.
Our wedding bed is open wide.
The Dead so quickly race,
We've reached our destined place."

Up to the gate of an iron fence
They rode with hanging reins.
With supple whip, a blow immense
Burst open bolt and chains.

The gate flew clattering open wide
And over graves, they rode inside,
The gravestones brightly beaming
With moonlight on them streaming.

Then suddenly her fears increase.
She stares with ghastly wonder.
The rider's armor, piece by piece,
Peels off and falls asunder.

As flesh fell off, so grew her dread.
A naked skull replaced his head.
Then, skeleton at last
With scythe and hourglass.

The horse drew short. It snorted, shied.
With scattering sparks it reared.
The ground beneath them opened wide
And down they disappeared.

A howling wail blared in the sky,
But, from the tomb, a whimpering cry:
Her heart, with trembling strife
Confronting Death and Life.

Nun tanzten wohl bei Mondenglanz,
Rundum herum im Kreise,
Die Geister einen Kettentanz
Und heulten diese Weise:

„Geduld! Geduld! Wenn's Herz auch bricht!
Mit Gott im Himmel hadre nicht!
Des Leibes bist du ledig;
Gott sei der Seele gnädig!"

□

The moonlight shone upon the ground
And on the airy throng.
The dancing spirits circled round
And sang the wedding song.

"Be patient, though your heart has pains.
Do not resist what God ordains.
Your body's reached its goal.
May God accept your soul."

□

Lurtsema

Lurtsema

Some years ago, at one of Adam and Marieke Weisblatt's lively parties at their home in Sudbury, Martin Slobodkin asked if I knew the shortest poem ever written. "It's called *Fleas*," I was told, "and the text goes 'Adam had'em'."

"Oh, I've got one shorter than that," I replied, and improvised the following.

# Terse Verse

I met the folksinger Jean Redpath in 1962, the year after she arrived in America from Scotland. And we became fast friends. Or maybe it's more like bantering buddies. She told me about a folksinging family she knew I would want to meet, "Fiddler" Bob Beers, his wife Evelyne, and daughter Martha. I saw them first performing on a stage in New York City. As usual, Jean was right. They were terrific. In no time at all, we were friends too.

Bob Beers invited me to visit an estate he had just purchased in Petersburg, New York. It was beautiful. A farmhouse in need of repair, but with great potential, and a few hundred acres of field and forest. He took me on a tour of some of the grounds, past a couple of frog ponds, to a low-lying hollow with a bog in the center and a sloping hill that rose gradually on three sides creating a natural amphitheatre.

"This is where we'll have the Festival," he said with a sweep of his hand, "once we clear away some of the trees and terrace the hillside. Up there," he pointed, "will be the crafts area. And down here," he said, pointing to the clump of reeds in the boggy area, "we'll put the stage."

Even as he said it, a red fox darted from the bushes and sped off into the forest. Without missing a beat, he said, "And we'll call it Fox Hollow."

He had a special way about him—a way that made people want to work with him, to be part of what he was doing. And he made them feel that what they were doing, however insignificant, was vitally important and appreciated. With the help of volunteers, including me, the Festival was ready the next summer.

It was a family festival. Folk singing families, friends of the Beers, came from all over the country, and other countries as well. And other families came to see them perform. There were no fences, no barriers, and no need for them. Except for when they were on stage, the performers were indistinguishable from the rest of the audience. People camped, endured downpours in the wet years and dust in the dry ones.

In between festivals, family, friends and performers would come for Thanksgiving, a long weekend of fun and frolic and feasting and swapping songs, and planning for next year's festival.

Then came that year when Bob was driving over to Williamstown for supplies—a trip I had made with him many times—only this time he didn't make it. No one knows exactly how the accident happened. But he was killed instantly.

We made a valiant effort to keep his spirit alive in the Festival that year and in the years to follow, but it never really was quite the same. For eighteen years I drove from Boston to Petersburg in early August, and finally it ended.

The year he died I wrote a song, but it was three years before I could sing it at the Festival. And even then emotion forced me to quit before I could reach the end.

Oh once I had a friend I
knew him ma - ny years and
ev - ery time I hear his name my
heart wells up with tears
fills right up with tears He could
play up a tune on a fid - dle or psal - te - ry
sang with a voice that was warm and strong all the
songs that he learned from his Grand - fa - ther Sul - li - van
He could sing them all day long.

## ❧ The Ballad of Robert Beers

Oh once I had a friend
I knew him many years
And every time I hear his name
My heart wells up with tears
Fills right up with tears

He could play up a tune on a fiddle or psaltery
Sang with a voice that was warm and strong
All the songs that he learned from his Grandfather Sullivan
He could sing them all day long

Oh the way he sang a song
Brought joy to people's ears
And after every song he sang
The room would fill with cheers
Fill right up with cheers

He would travel the country with Martha and Evelyne
Singing the songs that would bring them fame
Such as Dumbarton's Drums and the Seasons of Peace
And Fiddler's Green and the Golden Skein

Oh once I knew a man
His name was Robert Beers
And every time I think of him
The sadness reappears
Chokes my throat with tears

Every year we would go to his home for a festival
Banjos, guitars and pipes we'd bring
And the woods would resound with the sound of the music
And the families gathered there to sing

For they all knew the man
Or so it now appears
Whose memory would live with them
And brim their eyes with tears
Dim their eyes with tears

He was driving his car through the pass out of Petersburg
Driving over to Williamstown
On a treacherous stretch, no one knows how it happened, but
The road went up, his car went down

He's taken from us now
But each time summer nears
That special kind of warmth and love
Quickly reappears
Sadness disappears

There were Aarons and Bergers and Cadwells and Christensens
Olders, McCrearys, the family Perdue
Gramma Buckham, the Ushers, Boks, Beadnells and Carawans
Guy MacKenzie, Al Bluhm, an' the Young 'Uns too

They came from far and near
From different hemispheres
To share the camaraderie
Crew and volunteers
Band and balladeers

There were Armstrongs and Dildines and Trickets and Saletans
Hickersons, Burnstines, the Mitchells and Triers
There were Spences and Raineys and Patons and Nudelmans
Seegers and Ritchies and Boyers and Beers

And they still carry on
With all their singing peers
Fox Hollow still lives on and on
And will for many years
Will for years and years

□

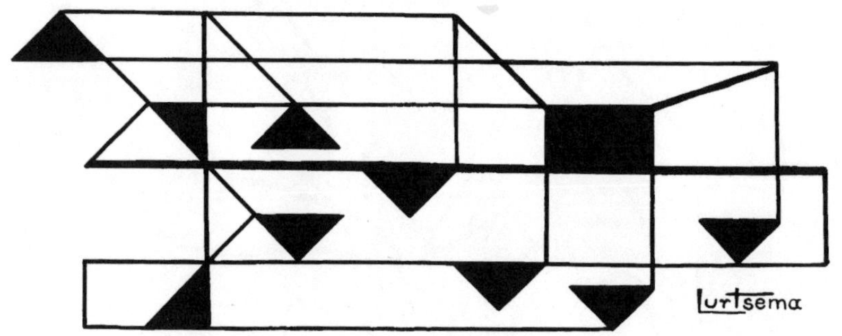


*F clef with notes*

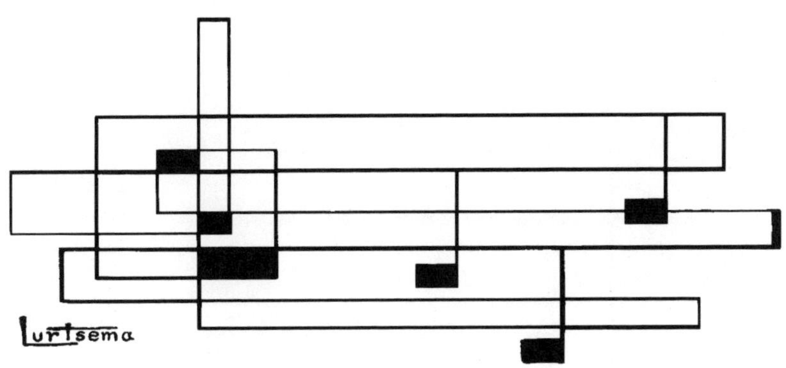


*G clef with notes*

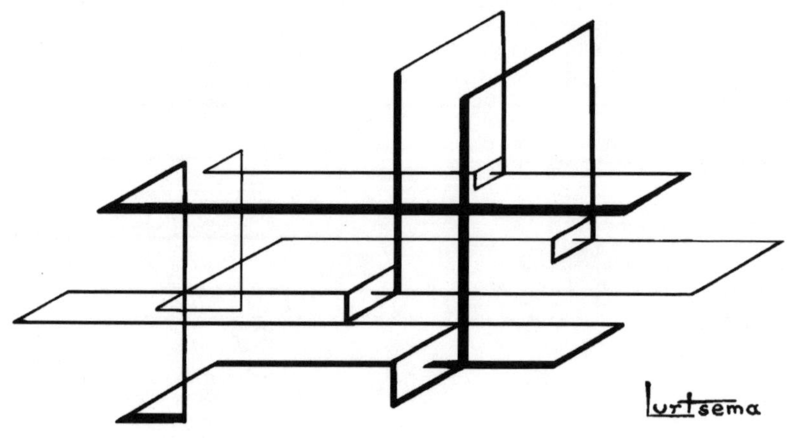


*counterpoint*

In 1975, composer Donald Harris came to the station for a conversation. We were featuring that morning a piece of music he had written, and he brought the score with him. The way we were positioned, it was more convenient for me to turn the pages. It wasn't very long before he remarked with astonishment, "You can't read music!" I admitted that, and added that what little I knew about music was self taught.

I told him that I had never had a formal course in music, and now in my fourth year as host of Morning pro musica I was over my head. It's tough to find answers if you're not sure which questions to ask.

As Vice President of the New England Conservatory, he was used to finding answers. A couple of weeks later, I received a letter signed by him and the Conservatory's President, Gunther Schuller, offering me a lifetime scholarship.

I began studying at the beginning of the next semester, and Donald Harris was my principal composition teacher. I majored in composition because it offered me the greatest opportunity for creativity and because I wasn't skilled enough on any one instrument.

To this day I carry in my wallet an NEC student I.D. card that reads, "Student in Perpetuity," which is how long I think they felt I would need to learn all I need to know.

Added to my good fortune was something that didn't happen every year. John Heiss, flutist, composer and teacher par excellence was teaching that year a course in instrumentation and orchestration. Each week we studied one instrument, wrote a piece for it and then got to hear how it sounded played in class by a fellow student.

We began with the woodwinds. My Opus One was a Caprice for Flute. I knew so little about scoring that I put the flags the wrong way on the eighth notes because I thought they should protect the note heads. The notes above the clef were meticulously placed without benefit of ledger lines. Somehow, Stephanie Jutt surmounted these and other obstacles and played it beautifully.

After the woodwinds, we went to the brasses. I was beginning to get the hang of it. I was even able to read some of what I was writing. When we reached the tuba, I wrote the following piece. The notation was still inaccurate, but a big improvement over Opus One. Non Troppo means "not too much." But I was thrilled when the copies of the score were returned to me after the class, and I found that one of my classmates had scrawled across the score, "Damn good!"

# NON TROPPO
## For Tuba, Op. 6

January 22, 1976

Robert J. Lurtsema

In early March of 1980, I was asked if I would "say a few words" at a benefit for the New England Conservatory. It was scheduled for Saturday, March 8th, at Quincy Market. I agreed, but gave it little thought until noon Saturday when I finished the program. I drove home thinking it might be nice to put a few thoughts in verse, something light and humorous.

I hadn't counted on the arrival of the Muse. But on she came, and with a vengeance. I had a vague idea of what I planned to write; she knew exactly what she wanted me to write. She won.

The result of the encounter was "The Dying Monk." And it was singularly inappropriate for the occasion. The hall was jammed with hundreds of Conservatory patrons. People chattered, waiters scurried, dishes clattered, I hurried.

Less than half the people could hear what I was saying, and not many of them were paying attention. I was so uncomfortable that it didn't occur to me that I could skip verses, and so I continued to the bitter end, secretly cursing my intrusive Muse.

In retrospect, I realize that she came along with the right idea at the right time. It was I who hadn't been able to come up with the right occasion.

## ❧ The Dying Monk

*In nomine Patris et*
*Filii et Spiritus Sancti . . .*

Is there a God? Have I grown so callous
That I could doubt my Teaching?
I've borne religion as a fragile chalice
Comforted by the preaching
Of Eternity's final palace.

Is there a God? Has it come to this
In the last few days of my years
Following Faith's own honied kiss
That I should have such fears
Forsaking Salvation's bliss?

Our youth is spent in search of Love's perfection
Chasing the banners of Hope.
In middle years, frustration and rejection
Instruct us how to cope.
In the end, there's just reflection.

Is there a God? How dare I ask?
And yet I know I must
See beyond that immortal mask
Where I have put my trust
As my final earthly task.

If God there is, then God of what?
Of Love, perhaps? When hate exists?
The concept is attractive, but
Not when War persists
And we're mired in conflict's rut.

If God there is, is God defined
As One devoid of caring,
As One who having shaped within our mind
Capacity for caring
Is heedless when we're unkind?

Perhaps a testing God, who keeps us all on trial
Instills a thirsting lust in us
For life, preparing all the while,
After all the fuss,
Death's ultimate denial.

Perhaps a tempting God, whose every exhortation
Compels pursuit of pleasure,
The satisfaction of sensation,
When in the end, the final measure
Is its own abrogation.

Perhaps a teasing God, who gives us just a taste
Of what might be, if only
Life were not a thing of haste
Where, in the end, and lonely,
Our dreams are laid to waste.

What of the God of Spring, when earth
Drinks rain, and there appears
The ritual stirrings of birth?
Here, in the winter of our years,
What is the springtime worth?

What of the God of Creative Perception,
Of Music, and Color, and Form?
Is the Muse of the artist's avid conception
Enough to keep our corpses warm
If Death is the final deception?

Can infinity be grasped by a finite mind?
Limitless Time and Space?
The indefinable finally defined?
When we reach that final resting place,
Is nothing-at-all all we will find?

Continually the numbers grow
Of starving people on earth.
Where did the God of Compassion go?
The God who perceives the dearth
Of feeling, and wills that it not be so?

Can I believe in a God who is blind
To the agonies of despair,
Put mankind's miseries out of mind,
Pretend that I don't care?
Is a God of Faith all that I'll find?

Is life, after all, a mere caprice?
So little time . . . the End is near.
I sense the approach of that final release.
Is it the revelation I fear?
Perhaps, the ultimate God . . . is Peace.

*In nomine Patris et*
*Filii et Spiritus Sancti . . . .*

□

## ❧ Some Lines Inspired by the Writings of Ogden Nash

It is not just an idle rumor
That most of the verses I write are laden with
side-splitting humor,

But for some reason I haven't deduced
No one seems prone to the paroxysms of laughter
to which they ought to have been reduced.

It is surely no fault of the writing
Which is often incisive and biting.

Deliciously honed for mirth,
But just when I'm expecting a plethora of
laughter, what I usually get is a dearth.

Cleverly constructed incongruities juxtaposed
in such a fashion that one couldn't prevent
oneself from instantly forgetting one's cares
Draw blank stares.

Lines that were written to leave them
rolling in the aisles
Don't even get smiles.

And it's not in the way that they're spoken.
It's just that those who are listening and
should be broken up with laughter,
somehow never seem to get broken.

When the humor is cleverly subtle
And I say to myself, "If that doesn't
get 'em, I don't know what'll:

I wait for a snicker.
Nary a flicker.

When the gags are dished up broadly enough so
that not even a diehard killjoy could quibble,
Still not a nibble.

Even when the subject is racy, which heaven
knows should get a response,
Only yawns.

There isn't even polite applause
For a line that should have caused guffaws.

So I guess I'll just have to take the advice I
recently received from a friend who said that if I
really want to pen material that will leave each
audience delirious,
I should write something serious.

□

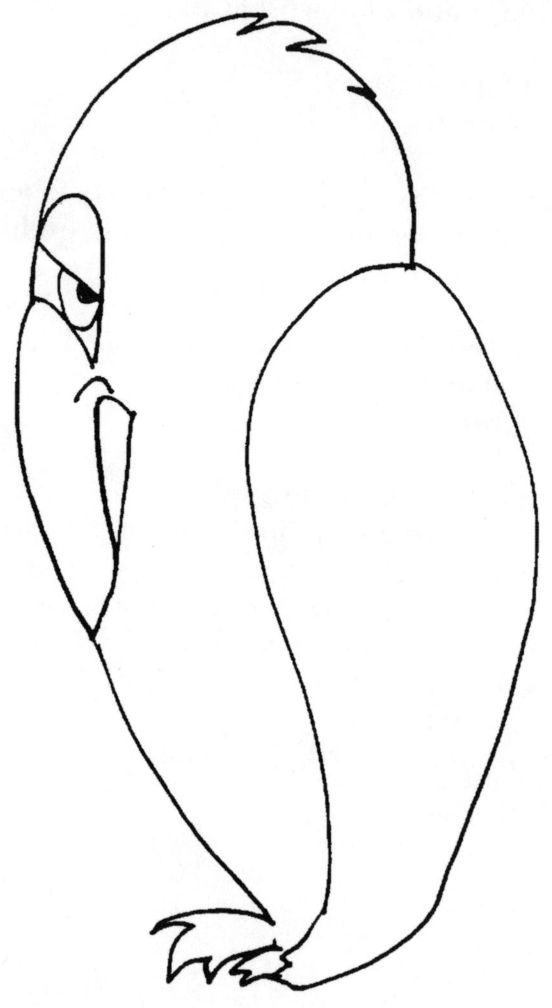

Sometime before October, 1971, when I switched from weekend to full-time host, Carol Langstaff, a folksinger I knew from the sixties, brought her father John Langstaff to the station. He talked with boundless enthusiasm about an idea he had for a pageant he called "The Christmas Revels." I couldn't have known it then, but in the years to come I was to play many roles in the Revels, performing in verse on stage and on many of the Revels records.

Some ten years later, Carol approached me with another project. She and others who were concerned about the possibility of nuclear warfare had been working on a film called "Button, Button . . . A Dream of Nuclear War." It was to be shown in Hanover, New Hampshire, August 12, 1982, and she wanted me to come and introduce it.

I agreed, and on the day of the event I drove up to Dartmouth and we met at the Hanover Inn for a mid-afternoon snack. William Sloane Coffin, who was to give the main speech, must have considered me completely antisocial, since I ignored him and everyone else as I worked feverishly on the text. I was still writing in the wings as Carol was introducing me from the stage.

The poem is designed to be read by two people (which is the reason for the italics), but on that night I read it alone.

## ❧ Button, Button

If survival is the answer
What is the question?
  *Button . . .*
If survival were the question
There could be no answer
  *Button, button . . .*
Can we afford extinction?
  *Who's got the button?*

The age old questions
Of what's beyond the outer edge of space
And what preceded the beginning of time
Give way to the puzzler of our own age,
Once everything is gone, what's left?
  *Hands . . .*
How much is enough?
  *Hands hovering . . .*
How much is enough once you exceed excess?
  *Too many hands hovering . . .*

Nuclear arsenal.
*New mown hay.*
Defensive capability.
*The colors of dawn.*
Window of vulnerability.
*A baby's fingernail.*
Radioactive fallout.
*Spring rain.*
Tactical weaponry.
*Fresh baked bread.*
Limited nuclear warfare.
*Music.*
Multiple warheads.
*A purring kitten.*
Ballistic missiles.
*The sound of surf.*
Nuclear parity.
*A sudden rainbow.*
Pre-emptive first strike.
*The joy of new love.*

Too many hands hovering on too many buttons.
*Can we afford to gamble the only planet we have?*
Is understanding unachievable?
*Is peace beyond our reach?*
When we, who reason, abandon discourse,
What is the value of intellect?
*What is the cost of civilization*
*If we sacrifice humanity?*
If survival is the answer
What is the question?
*Button . . .*
If survival were the question
There could be no answer.
*Button, button . . .*
Can we afford extinction?

□

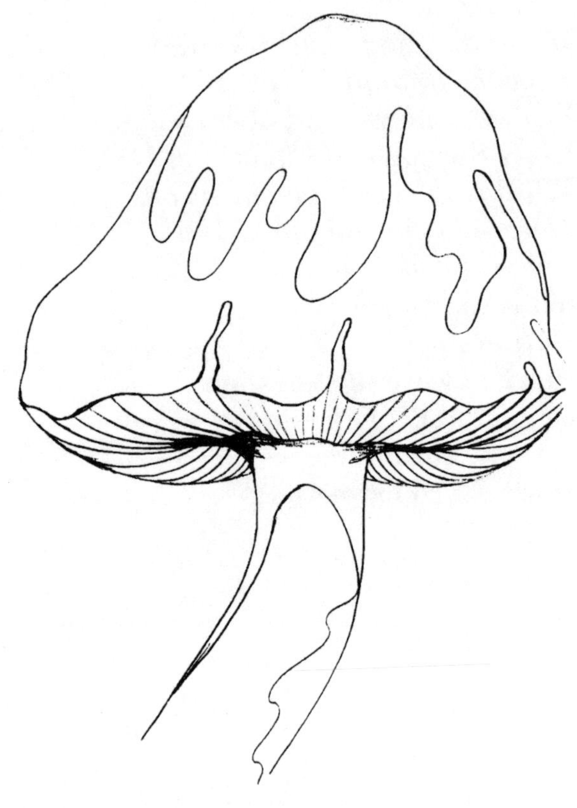

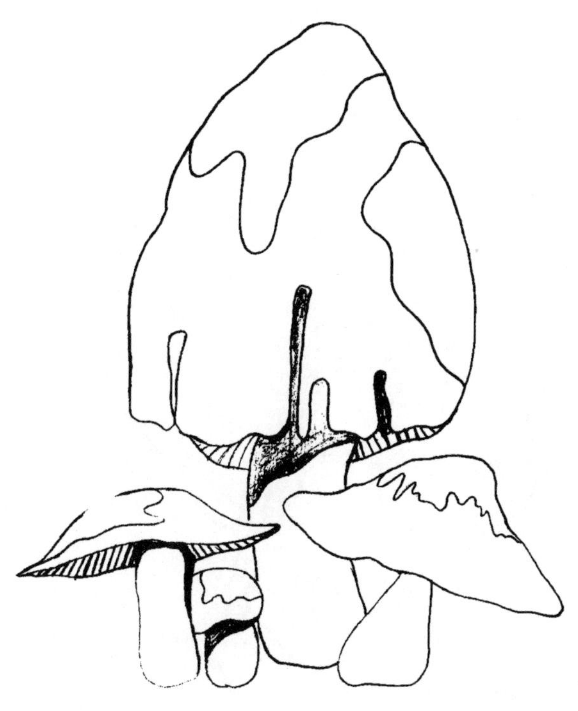

Deadlines are lethal. The ultimate deadline is the time after which inspiration is purposeless. That's what triggers the adrenalin. And adrenalin is the nectar of the Muse.

On a blistering day in August, 1983, the day the copy was due for my monthly column in Dial Magazine, I sat like a supplicant before my Royal Standard deity in the traditional writer's trance and stared at the page on which there were no words. "The pen is mightier than the sword," I thought.

Sword . . . words . . . hmmmm. . . . an anagram. . . .

And once again, the Muse was on a roll.

## ❧ Words

Words
Sword
Drows
Rowsd
Sowrd

Words
Words are toys,
things to play with,
play with, play on.
Played out?
Play on!
Plays are made of words,
and maids,
maids and pages.
Pages of words.
Blank pages
"Paging Words."
Blank. Blanks.
Blanket the page with words,
lines of words,
lifelines.

Deadlines
Lines dead,
Lines of communication.
Brain synapses with dead lines.
Sin napping.
Signals crossing.
Lines crossed.
Crosses.
Cross off days to deadlines.
Dazed and cross.
Deadlines are crosses to bear,
to bare.
Bare-brained
burdens of ambivalence.
Burr dens.
Nagging spurs of creativity.
Spur the nag
with words.
Words
Words are toys . . .

□

*Aaron Copland*

There are probably many different ways to talk with a guest on a radio show. But two approaches seem basic. In one, which I think of as "the Interview," the host asks questions from a previously prepared list of topics. The guest stays in the spotlight all the time, and a lot of information can be packed into a small period of time. But if the guest isn't naturally talkative, it can sound like an interrogation.

The second approach, which I think of as "the Conversation," is more give and take, and allows for an exchange of ideas that to me seems more natural. Listeners tend to feel they are eavesdropping. This approach is much harder to control, but can lead in directions the interviewer might not have thought to explore.

Over the course of twenty years, hundreds of guests have appeared for conversations "Live on pro musica." The list reads like a Who's Who of classical music. There have also been folksingers, dancers, comedians, environmentalists, authors, scientists, mimes, and many more.

When the great pianist Claudio Arrau came to the station for a conversation, we talked for a short while as the record was ending. Then I opened the mike, announced what the piece was, and we continued our conversation, a warm exchange of ideas that lasted for an hour.

As I was bringing the show to a close, he interrupted me a couple of times, and then after the network cue made it obvious that we had run out of time, he said with genuine disappointment, "I thought we were going to have an interview." The hour had gone by so quickly, and the conversation was so natural, that he hadn't realized we had been on the air all the time.

I first met Paul Winter when he arrived for a conversation in early November of 1982. The friendship that developed was so quick and fit so well it seemed to have been prepared ahead of time. In a sense, it was. We were both ardent environmentalists, and loved music, nature, adventure, and had so much more in common that an hour's conversation wasn't nearly long enough.

Paul had talked about wanting to find a place in Boston where he could present the New England premiere of Missa Gaia, the Earth Mass. So after the show and some lunch I took him around to churches and concert halls and finally to Symphony Hall, which seemed to be best suited for what he had in mind.

In April, I joined Paul and the Consort on a raft trip down the Colorado River through the Grand Canyon. We had seven rafts and 19 people sharing an adventure that ranged from the serenely beautiful to thrill-packed excitement. I can think of nothing on earth that compares with the splendor of the Grand Canyon. More adventures were to come, such as teaming up with our good friend Roger Payne to swim with the humpback whales, listening to their underwater singing off the coast of Hawaii, and visiting the crater of its famed Kilauea volcano.

When it came time for the performance of Earth Mass at Symphony Hall, Paul asked if I would introduce it. "The Earth Is Ours" was written October 21, 1983, for the performance the following night.

## ❧ The Earth Is Ours

In an outer arm
  of the galaxy,
Safe from harm,
  save for you and me,
A gem-like sphere
  of blue and white
Shines bright and clear
  in space-black night,
Spins 'round the sun
  that gave it birth,
"The Marbled One"
  our home,—the Earth.

From ground and granite
  It takes its name
This water planet
  with heart of flame,
  its soul ablaze.

We raise our voice
  in song of praise
As we rejoice
  In our land of dreams
With lakes and seas
  and hills and streams
With rocks and trees
  and grass and flowers
  and clean fresh air,
The Earth is ours,
  but just to share.

With wolf and whale
  and hunting fox
And garden snail
  and geese in flocks
With moray eels
  and dragon flies
And baby seals
  with soft wet eyes
With birds and bees
  and stalking cat
Algae and fleas
  and water rat
With nesting hen
  and busy ant
And canyon wren
  and elephant
With eagle, frog
  and nursing sow
Gorilla, dog,
  giraffe and cow
With lion, loon
  and sharks and minks
The masked raccoon
  the snake, the lynx
With bulls and bears
  with hound and hare,
The Earth is THEIRS
  as well, to share.

Along with leaf
  and bud and plants
We are but brief
  inhabitants
Dependent all
  on Earth—our mother
And, great and small,
  on one another.
From single cell
  to humankind
We must use well
  all that we find,
For Earth is still
  a finite source.

We have the will
  to set the course
To share, each day,
  with all our kin
That "fullness" for "they
  that dwell therein."
And heed the call
  of love and peace
As if we'd all
  co-signed a lease
For sun and showers
  and food and air,
The Earth IS ours,
But just to share.

□

I've always been fascinated by celestial phenomena. I learned the constellations and most of the major stars before I was in my teens, ground my own lens for an 8" telescope when I was 12, and saw the Northern Lights for the first time when I was 17, serving aboard a destroyer crossing the North Atlantic.

In 1970 it was my good fortune to be part of the Smithsonian team led by Dr. Menzel in Miahuatlan, Oaxaca, Mexico, for one of the most beautiful solar eclipses of the century. A total solar eclipse is one of nature's most awe-inspiring events, worth all the travel, inconvenience and expense that it usually takes to get to see one. I've been privileged to see six, including the second longest, off the coast of Senegal in 1974. Most recently, it was back to Mexico, to San Jose del Cabo, at the tip of the Baja peninsula for the longest eclipse of the century, July 11, 1991. It was spectacular!

Unlike Northern Lights and solar eclipses, Halley's Comet is something that happens only once in a lifetime, and I had been looking forward to it for a great many years. When it became apparent that the Northern Hemisphere was the wrong place to be for a good view, I headed for New Zealand.

Halley's Comet was still a fizz. Or more precisely, a fuzz. It was visible, but had no tail and didn't look much different from a nearby nebula. New Zealand, however, was a fantastic discovery.

From the Bay of Islands in the north, where it's warm, to the Southern Alps where it isn't, New Zealand is a land of incredible variety. Thermal springs at Rotorua with the world's largest boiling lake, fjords of unparalleled beauty such as Milford Sound, rain forests, glaciers, farms and deserts, mountains and towering waterfalls are all part of the diverse landscape. But it was a different kind of monument that inspired the following lines.

*The Rainbow Warrior*

## ❧ A Rainbow in Auckland

I stood on the dock in Auckland
  Waiting to hear a drum,
A bell, a gong, a trumpet,
  A sound that didn't come.
There was only the lap of the lazy tide
  And the traffic's steady hum
And nothing ceremonial.

I stood on the dock in Auckland
  Unexpectedly dismayed
By the lack of a plaque or a marker,
  Perhaps I'd expected displayed
Banners attracting attention
  And the sound of a grand parade
Something "76 Trombonial."

There by the dock in Auckland
  The dove was shining white
On the hull of the Rainbow Warrior
  And almost as if in spite
Of the bomb and the fire and sabotage
  The rainbow still was bright,
A silent testimonial.

□

Sometimes things are in your head for a long time, just waiting for that occasion for which they seem to have been saved. In January of 1988, I was driving down to Brown University in Providence, Rhode Island, for an appearance with the Charleston String Quartet at Brown University. It was a "Concert to End the Arms Race" to benefit the American Friends Service Committee.

Bouncing around in my brain on the way down were the words "What if the wind," a theme that often played itself in my head much as a snippet of melody comes and plays around with your mind without being invited.

"What if the wind . . .

What if the wind whispers?"—no, that wasn't it. That was picking up on T.S. Eliot's "The Hollow Men." I tried to put it aside, but still it nagged at me.

As I thought about the upcoming event, many of the pat phrases of the peace movement came to mind. "Give peace a chance." "Peace is the only way." By the time I got to Alumni Hall, "What if the wind" had changed to "What if the world," and the lines were falling into place.

It almost seemed to write itself, as if it had been there all along, just waiting for this event. By the end of the first string quartet, it was almost finished, and there was still another quartet left to polish it up.

## ❧ What if the World

What if the world said "No" to war
Demanded to know what the fighting was for
Then refused to accept the reason?

What if the world said "Yes" to peace
Insisted all conflict had to cease
And declared war "out of season"?

What if we really gave peace a chance
Chose not to march, when we could dance
And threw all the weapons away?

What if we all embraced the belief
That war doesn't solve, it causes the grief
And peace is the only way?

What if the world said, "Welcome, Friend,
Now that the arms race has come to an end,
Won't you take my hand?"

What if the people in every land
Worked with each other to understand
And framed an unrefusable demand
To give the concept of peace a chance to expand?
Sing in the streets with a big brass band,
"This is the way it should have been planned!"
Oh God . . . Wouldn't it be grand?
Wouldn't it? Wouldn't it be grand?

□

WGBH has a newsletter that they send out to contributors who are members of the "89.7 Club." Program hosts periodically are asked to contribute a message, an open letter, or an essay of one kind or another.

I was asked to write something that would reach the listeners around the middle of February, and got the idea of an open Valentine. The more I thought about it, the more intriguing it became.

The challenge for me was to write something that was generalized enough so that it would serve as a newsletter message to listeners without making them feel uncomfortable. But at the same time I wanted it to be intimate enough so that it could be sent—from one person to another.

## ❧ An Open Valentine

It isn't easy to define
But friendship's like a vintage wine
Improving with the years.
Yours means the world to me
And I gladly offer mine
With this, an open valentine
Unabashed as it appears,
Forthright as it can be.

To demonstrate how much it's meant
Each moment of the time we've spent,
To show how I appreciate
The kindnesses you've shown
The guidance and advice you've sent
The support and the encouragement
Until I could reciprocate
With something of my own.

Oh, there were times along the way
We put our tempers on display
Times when we could not agree
And lost patience with each other.
But "Time's a healer," so they say
And little by little, day by day,
Accepting the differences, we
Gained faith in one another.

And built a meaningful affair
With all the memories we share
And the comfort that comes from knowing
In times of need we can depend
On someone who is always there
Someone who will really care
With a love that keeps on growing
Whom we gratefully call a "friend."

□

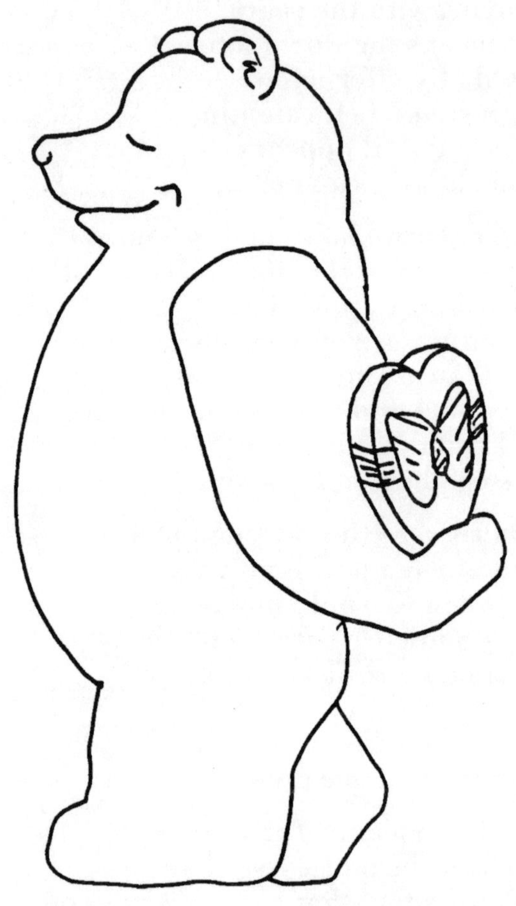

I am an inveterate doodler. A blank white surface is like an invitation. In restaurants where my predilection is known, I am often provided with extra placemats. (I bring my own pen.) Many of the drawings in this book are from the placemats salvaged by dinner companions, including the caricatures that follow. The verses that accompany them were written for this book while staying at the Cape Cod home of my good friends Bernie and Rory Greenhouse.

## *Carnival of the Critics*

He has two seats on the aisle
And there's nothing can beguile
Any hint of frown or smile
To give away

If the acting's great or stinks.
He just sits there like the sphinx
Not revealing what he thinks
About the play.

What he happily conceals
Puts the actors through ordeals
'Til he reveals the way he feels
And spoils their day.

She's the critic of the dance
She knows every small nuance
And she welcomes any chance
To vent her spleen.

As her eyes begin to glaze
She considers other days
Pirouettes and grand jetés
That might have been

If she hadn't been ignored
And her own career had soared.
Now she's old and plump and bored
And downright mean.

When you're roasting on the skewer
Of the noble book reviewer
Immolation flames as pure
As any pyre.

For his prose can be indicting
When he rates your strongest writing
Insufficiently exciting,
Lacking fire.

And you have no consolation
But that his denunciation
Proves he's lacking education
Or, a liar.

□

What's appealing to our eye
He will quickly pass right by
And if asked, he might reply
That it is quaint.

But he knows of countless ways
He can rapturously praise
What to us is just a maze
Of gucky paint.

He can deftly tear apart
Something painted from the heart
If we say we think it's art,
He'll say it ain't.

□

Not a note's beyond the sphere
Of the music critic's ear
For to him it's crystal clear
What it's about.

He can hear in any score
Things he never heard before
And if they're missing, what is more,
He'll point them out.

Though he doesn't want to bitch,
If he hears a tiny glitch
It exacerbates his twitch
And makes him pout.

□

Robert

It seems hard to believe, but over the course of my broadcasting career, I have given more than 30,000 newscasts. And at least that many times I have wondered about how the fate of an individual is determined by circumstances of birth.

Why, for example, should millions of children die of dehydration in an Ethiopian refugee camp before they are even old enough to comprehend the injustice?

What is the justification for the innocent victims of war, of Holocausts, or for the children who died of malnutrition by the hundreds of thousands in Biafra, or the peasant children of Bangladesh, drowned in the inevitable flood of the annual typhoon, or more recently children who are born drug-dependent or with AIDS or both.

When Ceausescu's "Curtain of Darkness" was finally lifted, the world had its first glimpse of Romania's ravaged economy and dispirited people, the rampant pollution, the exploited environment, the internal strife and most horrifying of all, the discarded children. Once seen, it was impossible to rid the mind of the horrifying images of children who were starving for life's basic necessities: food, affection and even such essentials of dignity as cleanliness, children who were relegated to orphanages and asylums with little to hope for but the release of death.

When the pianist Lory Wallfisch told me about a Smith College concert sponsored by the Free Romania Foundation to benefit the orphanages in Romania, and asked me to participate, I jumped at the opportunity. I looked through many sources for appropriate material, but found few poems that were sufficiently relevant. The search, however, was not wasted. On the drive to the concert I was able to write down some of what I had been trying to find.

I wasn't actually all that happy with it, feeling that it far too inadequately described what needed to be said. But since that first reading, April 30, 1990, "Suffer the Children" has been read at many other benefits, set to music, and even translated and published in Romania.

## ❧ Suffer the Children

"Suffer the children," the Saviour said
Suffering children whose parents are dead
"Suffer the children to come unto me."
Children of parents who fought to be free
In the North and the South, the East and the West
From Timisoara to Bucharest
Fought to fulfill a long cherished dream
Fought to tear down a repressive regime.
Fathers, husbands, mothers, wives,
Braving oppression, paid with their lives
For the values and principles each one held dear
So their children could live a life without fear
So their children could grow up with freedom of choice
With the freedom to move, and to give thought a voice
To battle oppression and rectify wrong
To join hands and dance and to sing a new song
A song of success they could sing far and near
An anthem of hope that would ring loud and clear.
But today's song's an old one we've all heard before
The dirge of the ravaged survivors of war
Of children whose parents are forever gone
Orphans of Fate who must still carry on.
"Suffer the children," the Scripture reads,
Destitute children with unfulfilled needs.
"Suffer the children to come unto me."
When will the children ever be free?
Suffer the children . . . . .

□

Orleans is a quiet town on Cape Cod, especially peaceful in wintertime, when the summer tourists are somewhere else. One event that livens it up is a series of lectures at Snow Library. I was asked by George Stierwald to participate in the 1990 series, with "a lecture, perhaps on classical music or broadcasting."

I said I wasn't a musicologist or a lecturer, and offered as an alternative a reading of poems, by some of my favorite poets, such as Frost and Eliot, and maybe a few of my own. My counteroffer was unusual enough to require an additional Board meeting. But the decision was favorable, and I was asked for the title of my talk. Since I hadn't given that any thought, I just said the first thing that came into my head, which was "A Pocketful of Verse."

As it turned out, the talk got postponed, and didn't actually happen until January 20, 1991. Typically, I waited until I was actually riding down to the Cape before I started to justify the title of my talk by expanding it into verse. I finished as we were pulling into the parking lot, where I took my scribbled notes and transcribed them into something I could read to open the "lecture."

There was a good turnout. Everybody seemed to enjoy the event, including me. In the question-and-answer period that followed, when I was asked if a book of my poems had been published, I explained that for me the joy was in the writing, and I was generally too busy responding to some other creative urge to think about the commercial aspects of what I had already done. Fortunately, there was in the audience a publisher, Trumbull Huntington. When I returned in May from a scuba diving trip to Cozumel, I found a letter from him explaining that his job *was* to think about the commercial aspects, and offering the services of Parnassus Imprints. And that's how this book came into being.

## ❧ A Pocketful of Verse

When I was not yet in my prime
I loved to join those childhood games
That all of us pursued
But often I would spend my time
Pursuing much more private aims.

Depending on my mood
I might try juggling or mime
Some concentrated skill that claims
A focused interlude.

I might converse all day in rhyme
Or learn a whole new set of names
In quiet solitude.

I'd learn the names of rocks and trees
How each bird sounds and how it flies
And then I would rehearse
And when I knew them all with ease
I'd find new lists to memorize.

I'd happily immerse
Myself in which plants lured the bees
And where the stars were in the skies.

One could do so much worse
Than travel with such friends as these
That one could rhyme or recognize
In a pocketful of verse.

□

# ❧ List of Poems